Hoover Institution Publications 147

The Strategic Land Ridge

THE STRATEGIC LAND RIDGE

Peking's Relations with Thailand, Malaysia, Singapore, and Indonesia

Yuan-li Wu

Hoover Institution Press
Stanford University
Stanford, California

Library of Congress Cataloging in Publication Data

Wu, Yuan-li.
    The strategic land ridge.

    (Hoover Institution publications ; 147)
    Bibliography: p.
    Includes index.
    1. China—Foreign relations—Asia, Southeastern.
2. Asia, Southeastern—Foreign relations—China.
I. Title. II. Series: Stanford University.
Hoover Institution on War, Revolution, and Peace.
Publications ; 147.
DS518.15.W8   327.51'059   75-12597
ISBN 0-8179-1471-4

Hoover Institution Publications 147
International Standard Book Number 0-8179-1471-4
© 1975 by the Board of Trustees of the
    Leland Stanford Junior University
Printed in the United States of America

Contents

Preface

This monograph, in a sense, is a sequel to the author's short study on *The Strategic Significance of Singapore,* published by the American Enterprise Institute in 1972. It is based primarily on current radio and news reports of a period about which few comprehensive works thus far have been published. Because of these sources and of space limitations, the study is only a small part of a long-range study program which the author has set for himself: namely, to examine the strategic, political, and economic interests of the United States—especially in the Western Pacific—in the new world environment of the 1970s and to observe the manner in which this new environment has evolved. Due to the timeliness of the subject, however, even such a limited account of contemporary history can serve a useful purpose. It can alert the reader to the inherent dynamics of major policy changes by big powers—changes that could slowly build up a momentum never before anticipated. The continuing "dialogue" between policy action and response across national boundaries is vividly illustrated by the many statements drawn upon in the monograph; they come from government officials, the press, spokesmen and mouthpieces of local insurgents. This manuscript was completed before the Indochina debacle of April 1975, which casts a special light on the discussion.

The author wishes to express his appreciation of the support of the Hoover Institution and its director, Dr. Glenn Campbell, for making the present undertaking possible. He is grateful to the many persons he met in the four countries discussed in this monograph for the insight they shared with him during personal discussions in 1970–71 and 1973. He wishes to acknowledge the research help he received from H. C. Ling, a long-time friend and colleague.

Yuan-li Wu

Menlo Park, California
November 1974

Introduction

Strategic Aspects of the Four-Nation Land Ridge

It is both risky and tempting to regard the phase of history in which one finds oneself as a critical turning point from which new and dramatic changes will ensue. It is even more tempting and dangerous to predict what these changes will be. These caveats notwithstanding, the first term of the Nixon Administration (1969–72) appeared to those who are interested in Asian affairs to be such a critical period. In an effort to end its involvement in the Vietnam War and—some would say—to use rapprochement with Peking as a means toward this end and a way to redress the precarious power balance against Moscow, during this period the United States initiated a dynamic process of international realignment from which few nations are likely to emerge unaffected.[1] It is even possible that the American effort to seek a new viable position in a stable global equilibrium (yet to be established in Asia as of this writing[2]) *may* end in the virtual liquidation of its preeminent position. This position was acquired at the end of World War II and the Korean War.

The accent should be on the word "may," however. The ultimate outcome of the continuing adjustments is not independent of the policies of many large and small nations—which are by no means predetermined—and of random, exogenous events. We cannot foretell, for example, what the United States or the Soviet Union will do during the Ford Administration; or whether internal affairs in mainland China, rapidly coming to a head in the mid-1970s, may not totally unhinge certain key parameters of the process of adjustment. It is undeniable that during the middle third of the 1970s, however, we are increasingly witnessing in Asia some of the effects of Nixon's first-term Asian policy.

This process of policy adjustment and interaction is a most inter-

1

esting one to observe. In addition, the account of this process provided in these pages serves several utilitarian purposes: as chronicles
for the future historian, as an analysis for policy-makers who still
find the time and have the inclination to contemplate, and as reading
material for students who are curious to know how things came to
pass in certain parts of Asia during this period.

As indicated in its title, this monograph will limit itself to a study
of only one principal aspect of the process of policy adjustment of
four Asian nations (Thailand, Malaysia, Singapore, and Indonesia)
following and, to a significant degree, as a result of the rapprochement between Washington and Peking and the disengagement of
U.S. forces from Vietnam. The principal questions are how these
four nations have adjusted their relations with mainland China and
how the People's Republic of China (PRC) and the local communist
parties have acted in the four countries.

These are not idle questions for the following reasons:

First, as the traveler moves south from Thailand down the Malaysian Peninsula to Singapore, he is crossing a land bridge from the
Asian mainland to the Indonesian archipelago. The PRC, a land
power, provides an extreme example of the intense political interest in
this area through its deep involvement with the Indonesian Communist Party (PKI) up to the eve of the Chinese Cultural Revolution[3] and
through the Indonesian communists' abortive coup in October 1965.
Chinese support for local communist parties and the presence of
large ethnic Chinese groups in all four countries suggest that Peking
could well regard this "land bridge" as a natural gateway to Southeast Asia and beyond. It offers the PRC a "comparative advantage"
not available either to Washington or to Moscow. So long as the
Chinese Communists do not possess an ocean-going navy, this land
route and the immediate coastal waters might appear to Peking to
provide easier accessibility to local insurgency than any other means
should the Chinese desire to supply such insurgents with material
support.

Second, the four countries, together with Burma, historically con-
stituted the principal western land border of Japan's expansion in
World War II. The economic significance to Japan of the area's
natural resources was graphically illustrated during the 1973 Arab
oil boycott in light of the proven oil reserves of Indonesia and the

potential reserves lying offshore from the Southeast Asian mainland and islands.[4] Undoubtedly a major motivating factor in Japan's World War II plans in this region was the quest for markets and for raw materials, including but no means limited to oil. The economic importance of this area to Japan is further enhanced by the far greater economic stature to which Japan has risen since World War II and its consequent demand for natural resources to sustain the present high level of economic activity and the continuation of the country's economic growth. While only a relatively small proportion of Japan's raw material import is now derived from this area, the region constitutes a major source of future expansion.[5] Proximity, which implies both lower costs and potentially greater security of supply for shipments enroute, will be of primary importance to Japan. The area can also be used as "staging places" for raw materials originating elsewhere, e.g., storage and refining of Middle Eastern oil in Sumatra. Japan's experience in the 1973 "oil shock" made this situation amply clear. If Japan is to become an important contributor to stability and progress in any part of the world, its expanded economic cooperation with these land-ridge nations is absolutely essential.

Another factor of concern is the indirect impact of Japan's economic vulnerability on the strategic balance involving the super powers. When the Arab exporting countries imposed their oil embargo on Japan in late 1973, Tokyo authorities were compelled to bow to the Arab demand that Japan publicly alter its official attitude toward Israel.[6] Armed with offers of capital, equipment, and technology, several top Japanese officials embarked upon tours of many Arab nations in order to express Japan's friendly disposition toward them. This readiness of Japan to buckle under extreme economic pressure could well indicate the shape of things to come. As stated by the *Mainichi* in its 1974 New Year's Day editorial, the oil crisis and the prospective shortage of other raw materials were, for Japan, "almost as grave as being defeated in war." If defeat in war could lead to surrender, as it did in World War II, then the same could happen again. "The Japanese must draw a distinct line between what they really need and what is desirable for them," said *Mainichi*. "We must secure materials and goods really necessary for Japan and the Japanese *at all costs* [italics added], but we should curb our desire."[7]

The cost could be a radical shift of policy in favor of whatever country or countries might be capable of turning off the flow of supplies at source or of threatening to disrupt the vital sea lanes over which supplies are transported to the Japanese home islands. Three of the four countries under study—Singapore, Malaysia, and Indonesia—could exercise direct influence over several key straits and are, therefore, important by virtue of their indirect influence on the position of Japan in the world's strategic balance.[8] Each of the super powers in turn must decide whether it desires to see Japan allied, or continue to be allied, with one or more of its major potential adversaries and what it proposes to do about the matter.

In the third place, the Malaysian peninsula, in conjunction with the Indonesian islands, is a land ridge separating the Indian and Pacific oceans. Control of the gateways through this land ridge, including the vital Malacca and Lombok straits, and of the land ridge itself, could give a Pacific Ocean power a major role in the Indian Ocean or an Indian Ocean power a substantial voice over Pacific Ocean affairs. If assured of free passage through the strategic straits, a strong maritime power can aspire to complete domination of both the Indian Ocean and the western Pacific. It is only too obvious that such a maritime dominance leads to strategic and political influence over (a) the large littoral states, including the Chinese mainland, the Indochina peninsula, and the Indian subcontinent, and (b) the island chain of nations south of the Korean peninsula. (Australia can be included under either (a) or (b).)

A special role has fallen on the modern navy due to conditions of mutual strategic nuclear deterrence based on mutual vulnerability between the United States and the Soviet Union. The situation was, as it were, "codified" by the Nixon–Brezhnev strategic arms agreements of 1972, reinforced in 1974 by the Ford–Brezhnev talks at Vladivostok. Any nation dominating the land ridge and the gateways cutting through it could reinforce its maritime dominance with land-based air and coastal forces. Control of the land ridge by an adversary, however, could dilute the naval dominance of the maritime power. From the point of view of overflight, the land ridge also has significance.

These are important geo-political considerations for the Soviet Union whose marked naval expansion in recent years, including increasing presence in the Indian Ocean and growing fleet activities in the Pacific, indicates a level of aspiration exceeding that of the United States after World War II. While the U.S. Seventh Fleet—at no time particularly active in the Indian Ocean—is concentrated in waters east of Malacca, the Soviet Union seems intent on filling the vacuum left by the British and threatens to be quite successful. An ocean-girding naval arc from Odessa to Vladivostok will be in the making if settlement of the Arab-Israeli War of 1973 should eventually entail the reopening of the Suez Canal—incidentally, with both Soviet and Japanese aid—thus making the Indian Ocean directly accessible to the Soviet fleet based in the Black Sea. Control of the particular land ridge under consideration thus could assume a special meaning in both Soviet and U.S. strategic planning.[9]

In general terms, a corollary to the preceding geo-political considerations concerns the usefulness of the Bay of Bengal and its adjacent waters as the hunting ground of ballistic missile submarines aimed at Soviet and/or mainland Chinese targets. Any support or hindrance provided to these special naval vessels by the Thailand–Malaysia–Singapore–Indonesia land ridge obviously will have at least a marginal influence on the overall U.S.–Soviet–PRC strategic balance.

Finally, the importance of the four "land ridge" nations must be examined in the light of the post-Vietnam policy of the United States. One important outcome of the disengagement of U.S. forces from Indochina is the fact that Thailand, northernmost of these four countries, is the only nation in mainland Asia other than South Korea where U.S. forces are still stationed today (1974). Their purpose is ostensibly to police the Indochina cease-fire which has never really been observed. Hence, whither Thailand goes will be a test of the viability of a U.S. policy that hopes to help maintain stability in the region at a lower level of U.S. military involvement.[10] Furthermore, during the period when America's military presence in Indochina was being scaled down, U.S. authorities were inclined to speak of greater U.S. economic involvement in Southeast Asia and the consequent increase in prosperity and economic interdependence this would create. Greater economic development and interdependence with the West, of which Japan and the United States are regarded as integral parts reinforcing each other, would then serve as a bulwark against communist subversion and insurgency.

Japan's behavior under Prime Minister Tanaka during the 1973 energy crisis seriously undermined the degree of confidence placed in its ability to act alone as a stabilizing force. Through riots and student demonstrations in 1973–74, both Thailand and Indonesia exhibited popular resentment of serious proportions against Japanese economic behavior. Japan's future raw materials policy may either expand or reduce these expressions of Southeast Asian economic nationalism. However, the role a greater U.S. economic presence, augmented by U.S.-Japanese economic cooperation, is supposed to play in the face of U.S. military withdrawals from mainland Asia and the general deterioration of the American strategic position as a super power may be seriously undermined by both local and Japanese economic nationalism and possible rivalry between individual U.S. and Japanese business interests.

Recapitulating the above factors:

(1) Control of the land ridge from mainland Asia southward and of the straits across it is of vital importance to any maritime power aspiring to dominate both the Pacific and the Indian oceans. Hence, the land ridge countries are natural "target countries" of Soviet, PRC, and U.S. policies.

(2) This land ridge controls vital sea lanes supplying Japan. Its control by any major power or, conversely, its susceptibility to disruption by a major power, could be used as effective leverage against Japan, although the same essential sea lanes could also be threatened farther to the north of Indonesia or west of the Malacca Straits. The attitude of three of the four countries (i.e., excluding Thailand) thus can exert a strong indirect influence on the future alignment of Japan.

(3) The land ridge also constitutes a "land bridge" which could link mainland China to the Indonesian archipelago. A decisive step toward the establishment of such a link would have been successfully taken had the Peking-supported PKI coup of October 1965 resulted in communist control of Indonesia. In the future, should a strong PRC succeed in establishing itself as the dominant influence across this land bridge, it would be better able to sway the external alignment of Japan. In the remote chance that Japan could be persuaded to move closer to the PRC under such conditions, the latter thereby will have interposed a powerful third force which could tilt the balance between the United States and the Soviet Union.

(4) In the wake of U. S. disengagement from Indochina, Thailand —as the northernmost country on this land ridge—is far more exposed than the other three. All four, however, are subject to potentially greater pressure from both Communist China and the Soviet Union, the former by virtue of proximity. The 1973 Arab oil embargo against the Western powers and Japan produced a graphic illustration of the relative short-run powerlessness of the embargoed nations despite their status as major oil producers (or concessionaires) and consumers. A serious question raised by this experience is the degree of political benefit in using pure economic presence as a means of influence on the foreign policy of another country. In both economic and non-economic terms, the effectiveness of U. S. as well as Japanese economic presence could be seriously undermined by mutual economic and business rivalry. Such rivalry may be aggravated by the quest of both to enlarge each nation's own energy supplies in reaction to the 1973 crisis.

Accordingly, at a given lower level of U. S. military and political influence unsupported by a rising complementary influence from Japan, the most important external factor affecting this area's future will be the *net* influence of the two major communist powers. While the latter now act in opposition to each other, the possibility of their acting in concert must also be considered. Opposed to this external influence is the force of political and economic nationalism of the countries in question. As long as Sino-Soviet rivalry continues, the net communist influence is reduced and the strength of the resistance by local nationalism against each communist power is increased. Since it is natural for the local nationalist to try to balance the presence and influence of each major communist power by its rival, his receptivity to Soviet overtures may be a function of his assessment of the growth of Peking's influence, and *vice versa*. This makes examination of the interactions between Peking, on the one hand, and Bangkok, Kuala Lumpur, Singapore, and Jakarta, on the other, even more interesting and meaningful than they would otherwise be.

Policy Interaction with Peking

Two sets of major benchmarks should be borne in mind in examining the evolution of the policies of Peking and the Southeast Asian countries toward each other and the process of policy interaction involving the principal interested powers. The first concerns Peking's general domestic and foreign policy developments, while the second is dominated by the evolution of a new U.S. policy toward Communist China.

Immediately before the onset of the Cultural Revolution (1966–69), Peking's policy was dominated by that of Liu Shao-ch'i. The Chinese economy had just recovered from the depths of a depression (1960–61) and was again ready for a major push forward. Recovery was engineered by abandonment of Maoist radicalism introduced during the Great Leap (1958–59) and by loosening of centralized controls. This "relaxation" apparently went beyond the long-term norm tolerable to the Maoists and could justifiably be described by them as "revisionist." Had the Cultural Revolution not intervened, the Chinese economy theoretically could have followed two alternative non-Maoist paths: (a) a more revisionist path characteristic of the recovery period; or (b) a better coordinated but more centrally planned system characteristic of the first Five Year Plan (1953–57) and of the initial phase of the second plan (originally scheduled for 1958–62 but overtaken by the policies of the Great Leap).

In practice—although this is speculating on what might have been—PRC authorities probably would have eschewed either of the "pure" or "idealized" forms and the world might have seen a pragmatic admixture of both. In this connection, "pragmatism" would have been defined by internal economic as well as political considerations. Such an economy would probably have been more efficient and more able to support Peking's external policies. In general terms, these external policies on the eve of the Cultural Revolution were characterized by (a) continued Sino-Soviet rivalry contained within certain limits, (b) hostility toward the United States, and (c) in the geographical area of our present interest, a significant degree of aggressive militancy through support of local revolutionary groups and, possibly, even expansion.

Thus, insofar as Peking is concerned, distinction should be made between a pre- and post-Cultural Revolution period. Veiled ideological attacks on Liuist (i.e., Liu Shao-ch'i) revisionism had already begun in the winter of 1965-66. The Cultural Revolution, with its rampaging Red Guards and frequently untrammeled attacks on established institutions and figures of authority, reached its height during 1967–68. This period of domestic disruption on the Chinese mainland was also a period of ineffectual diplomacy by Peking and its virtual isolation from the rest of the world. If the radical ideas espoused by domestic extremists were echoed by fanatic militancy in the PRC's external dealings in certain countries—e.g., in Africa[11]— this radicalism was more than tempered by ineffectual performance. Hence, for our purpose, the Cultural Revolution could be treated as an interval of policy suspension.

It is difficult to say when the Cultural Revolution ended or when Peking's policy of rapprochement with the United States began. A plausible date for the former would be the early spring of 1969 when the Ninth Congress of the Chinese Communist Party was convened and Lin Piao was named heir to Mao in the new party constitution. This conference followed, and partially coincided with, several sharp military clashes with Soviet forces on the border. Peking's new policy toward the United States was tentatively announced two years later. While the American ping-pong team was playing at a tournament in Japan, it was invited to visit Peking. An intensive internal policy debate doubtless took place during the two-year interval preceding this invitation, overlapping a power struggle for succession to the top leadership. These two years thus may be regarded as the first phase of the post-Cultural Revolution period, to be separated from the "post–ping-pong" phase which has continued into the present (mid-1974).

Concerning U. S. policy, the principal benchmarks follow: (a) 1965 was the year when the United States began the major build-up of its forces in Vietnam; (b) 1969 saw the first faint indication of what was to become a new China policy in the form of some minor relaxation of restrictions on travel by Americans to mainland China. In this context, the pre-Nixon period (1965–69) was the last phase of the Dulles foreign policy which had been based on unchallenged U. S. strength, albeit eroded considerably after 1962, and a world-wide alliance system.

The Nixon period, with a policy of trying to create stability through an artificially-engineered and hoped-for balance of power, until 1974 was punctuated by several additional benchmarks: (a) July 1971, when President Nixon announced his acceptance of Chou

En-lai's invitation to visit Peking; (b) October 1971, when the PRC won the China seat in the United Nations at the expense of the Nationalists' Republic of China; (c) February 1972, when Nixon visited Peking and a Joint U.S.–PRC Communiqué was issued in Shanghai; (d) March 1973, when the United States completed its military withdrawal from Vietnam. Other events, including the establishment of liaison offices by the two countries in each other's capitals and the signing of the Vietnam cease-fire in January 1973, were additional landmarks in the deliberately staged rapprochement between Peking and Washington.

Since the evolution of U.S.–Peking relations is expressly designed by the United States to progress by stages, additional landmarks can be anticipated. Their exact nature and timing, however, do not seem to be fully determined. Furthermore, one must envisage a post-Nixon period no less than one must allow for a post-Mao and post-Chou period. Continuity of national foreign policies is based upon the continued existence of certain policy parameters, if not upon individual policy-makers. The attitudes and policies of Southeast Asian nations are, of course, among these policy parameters. The succession of President Ford to Mr. Nixon may soon be followed by a change of guard in Peking.

If the two sets of benchmarks are lined up along the two sides of a time axis, the divisions on the chart on the facing page can be made. Abstracting the Cultural Revolution period itself, U.S. and PRC policies of the pre-Nixon and pre-Cultural Revolution periods can be readily illustrated by the state of affairs in 1965. Thus, this year may be regarded as the starting point of our analysis.

The Nixon period can be divided into two phases more sharply on the Chinese side than on that of the United States. Phase One (Spring 1969–Summer 1971) is a period of intense policy debate and internal struggle. Phase Two, in which we still find ourselves, dates from the summer of 1971 and is the current period of PRC accommodation to U.S. policy, as well as the period of U.S. force reductions in Asia.[12]

The Pre-Nixon period

The Nixon period

Year		
	Pre-Cultural Revolution policy	U.S. force buildup in Vietnam
1965		
1966		
1967	Sino-Soviet border clashes	
1968		
1969	9th CCP Congress and end of Cultural Revolution	Nixon's relaxation of travel restrictions to the PRC
		Guam Speech
1970		
1971	Invitation to U.S. ping-pong team	Nixon's acceptance of Chou's invitation
	Fall of Lin Piao	PRC admission to UN
1972		Nixon's visit to Peking and Shanghai communique
1973	A second "Cultural Revolution?"	Completion of U.S. withdrawal from Vietnam
1974		

Post-Nixon
?

The Cultural Revolution

Peking Policy debate on U.S. relations

The Post-Cultural Revolution Period

Post-Mao and Post-Chou
?

Abstracting the Cultural Revolution period itself, U.S. and PRC policies of the pre-Nixon and pre-Cultural Revolution periods can be readily illustrated by the state of affairs in 1965. Thus, this year may be regarded as the starting point of our analysis.

The Nixon period can be divided into two phases more sharply on the Chinese side than on that of the United States. Phase One (Spring 1969–Summer 1971) is a period of intense policy debate and internal struggle. Phase Two, in which we still find ourselves, dates from the summer of 1971 and is the current period of PRC accommodation to U.S. policy, as well as the period of U.S. force reductions in Asia.[12]

— 1 —

PRC–Thailand Relations

The Pre-Cultural Revolution and Pre-Nixon Period

Two major themes ran through PRC statements concerning Thailand before and during 1965. First, in Peking's view, Thailand was becoming increasingly involved in the Vietnam War. Bangkok was accused of acting under the orders of the United States. The penalty for such a policy was internal revolution. Second, the United States was regarded as aggressively active. "U. S. imperialism" thus had to be defeated and thrown out of Indochina.

On April 28, 1965, the New China News Agency (NCNA) stated through its commentator that U. S. imperialism was making increased use of Thailand as a base for extending the war in Vietnam and that Washington was trying to dragoon Thailand into America's aggressive war. Several months later, on September 10, 1965, the *People's Daily* (Peking) noted that Thailand had repeatedly vilified and threatened Cambodia "at the instigation of the United States." On October 7, quoting the *People's Daily,* NCNA warned the Thai authorities against political miscalculation. "It is certain," wrote the official organ of Peking, "that the wider the Thai authorities throw open the door to the American wolves and turn the country into a new-style colony and military base of the United States, the more widespread and intensified will the patriotic struggle become in Thailand. The Thai people will never allow the Bangkok rulers to push their country into the abyss of despair by serving the United States policies of aggression and war. The Thai authorities must stop at once their criminal acts of following the United States in its

13

aggression against Vietnam and the whole of China. Otherwise, they will meet with the same shameful end as the U. S. aggressors."

This official Peking position was shared by two Chinese front organizations, the Patriotic Front of Thailand (PFT) and the Thailand Independence Movement (TIM).[13] At its first anniversary on November 1, 1965, the latter echoed the earlier official Chinese position. Referring to the intensified military participation of Thailand in the Indochina War, the statement declared, "In this situation we must unite on a broad scale and expand our forces, to drive out U. S. imperialism and overthrow the dictatorial and traitorous regime of Thanom and Praphat. Only so can our country recover its independence and advance along the road of democracy, peace, neutrality, and prosperity." The TIM spokesman also took pains to point out that the "revolutionary struggle of the Thai people" had already extended to every corner of Thailand.

An example of the degree of coordination between Peking and Thai revolutionaries under the banner of these movements was provided by NCNA over whose stations a PFT statement of September 1, 1965, was broadcast on November 8 of the same year. This declaration denounced the Thanom government for "selling-out the land in Northeast Thailand to U. S. imperialism as a military base for aggression against neighboring countries and for sending police on mopping-up operations in the Northeast and killing people there." According to the Front, "The enemy's suppression will not be confined to the Northeast region alone." It also appealed to "all forces in Thailand" to follow the example of the "self-defense struggle" of the people in the Northeast.[14] Peking accused the Thai Prime Minister of having had secret talks with the Saigon government in Bangkok. A statement was attributed to the Thai Foreign Minister to the effect that Chinese nationals in Cambodia were receiving training in guerrilla warfare in order to help the Vietcong, thus endangering the security of Thailand.[15] The Peking influence on Thai insurgents was thus more than a little evident although—like insurgency elsewhere— that of Thailand was born of, and nurtured by, long-standing grievances at home.[16]

The Post-Cultural Revolution and Nixon Period

Attitude of the PRC and Thai Communists

The Cultural Revolution and the passage of three years since 1965 had had very little effect on PRC–Thai relations. Quoting the Voice of the People of Thailand (VPT), a clandestine radio broadcasting from China, NCNA reported on January 11, 1969, a statement of the Communist Party of Thailand (CPT) which called upon the Thai people "to resolutely carry out the people's war so as to drive the U. S. imperialist aggressors out of Thailand and overthrow the traitorous Thanom–Praphat clique which brings ruin to the people and to the country." If this was not sufficient to demonstrate the CPT's Maoist position, the statement also referred to Mao's now famous saying that political power grows out of the barrel of a gun and that the seizure of power by armed force and the settlement of national issues by *war* are the *central tasks and the highest form of revolution.*

The VPT mentioned in the same statement that the Thai Communist Party had waged revolutionary war for more than three years, thus placing the *official beginning* of the *insurgency in Thailand in 1965,* the year large-scale participation of the U. S. forces in the Vietnam war began. Evidence of insurgent activities was often reported by non-communist sources. According to the *Bangkok World* of January 8, 1969, for example, a communist arms cache with uniforms and Mao badges was discovered in Loei Province. The arms hoard was reported to contain a large number of carbines, and over twenty communist terrorists' uniforms and Red Chinese military insignia were found among the weapons.

On March 7, 1969, NCNA again quoted an article of the VPT which expressed "resolute support for the just act of the Chinese people and armed forces in defense of the territorial sovereignty of their motherland." This time, however, the Thai Communist Party was putting itself on the side of the Chinese Communists against the

Soviet Union. The Soviet "revisionist renegade clique" was now said to be "the chief accomplice of U. S. imperialism." Following the same line, a VPT broadcast in Thai declared on March 12, 1969:

The Communist Party of Thailand and the Thai revolutionary people strongly condemn this trick [i.e., the Soviet–PRC clash on the Chen-pao or Damanskyi Island, which was said to be a Soviet conspiracy or "trick" in collusion with the United States against Peking] and the base crimes of the Soviet clique. They fully support every measure adopted by the CPR to safeguard its sovereignty. The Communist Party of Thailand considers support for and defense of the CPR, the bastion and most honest and reliable friend of the revolutionary people of the world, to be an *international duty* [italics added]. The communiqué issued on the twenty-fourth anniversary of the Communist Party of Thailand states that one duty of the revolutionary people, including the Thai, is to fight side by side with the Chinese people, to protect People's China from being destroyed by the foreign imperialists, reactionaries, and revisionists. The Communist Party of Thailand appeals to all party members and revolutionary people to fully support the Chinese people in protesting and fighting against the Soviet revisionists.

President Nixon was not to escape the venom of the VPT, hence indirectly of NCNA. Broadcasting in Thai on March 17, 1969, the VPT accused Americans, and especially President Nixon, of an intention "to use Asians to kill Asians." In doing so it anticipated a later theme of communist propaganda against the "Nixon Doctrine" and "Vietnamization" of the Indochina War.

It is also alleged that the Acting Director General of the Information Department of the Thai Foreign Ministry had said that Taiwan representatives should be allowed to observe a SEATO (Southeast Asia Treaty Organization) Council meeting scheduled to be held in Bangkok around mid-May 1969. "The recognition of Taiwan, a province of China, as an area under SEATO, an aggressive tool of imperialism," commented the VPT, "shows that the U. S. imperialists have arrogantly demonstrated their aggression against and their defiance of the CPR and that the fake Thanom government, the chief promoter of SEATO, desperately pursues an anti-China policy, on orders from the U. S. imperialists."

This strong anti-U.S., anti-Soviet, and anti-Thai government attitude continued through mid-year 1969, beyond the Ninth Party Congress in Peking. On July 1, 1969, the VPT again accused the Soviet Union and Thailand of collusion against the insurgents. Referring to reports in U.S. newspapers published in Thailand, it alleged that "officials of the Soviet revisionist renegade clique in Thailand [had] made trips to various 'dangerous areas' in the country without any reaction from the Thanom–Praphat clique. This means that the clique has allowed the Soviet revisionists to make inspection tours of areas where the people's arms struggle is active, as well as into various sensitive areas." According to the VPT, this showed that the Russians were collaborating with the U. S.–Thanom clique in order "to put out the flame of the people's armed struggle."

Referring to the then Thai Foreign Minister, the VPT said that Dr. Thanat had once disclosed a promise made by the Soviet government some time earlier to use its influence to avoid any communist threat against Thailand. The Thai Prime Minister, according to the VPT, had said that the Thai government was willing to receive Soviet military aid. On the following day, July 2, 1969, the VPT repeated its accusation that the Soviet Union was becoming more active in Thailand and had increased its collaboration with the Thai government. It added that the Soviet Union was trying to induce various Southeast Asian countries to form a so-called "joint defense organization to oppose China."

Orchestration of denunciations of this alleged anti-Peking Soviet theme was conducted by NCNA, which mentioned on the same day that the Soviet Union was frantically opposing China and was trying to "rig-up a so-called system of collective security in Asia." According to NCNA, the proposed Soviet system of collective security in Asia was practically the same thing as the "aggressive military bloc rigged-up by U. S. imperialism." It was a *Soviet* attempt to bring about "*a ring of encirclement against China* [italics added]." NCNA then referred to Soviet policy "to suppress the revolutionary armed struggle" of the Asian, African, and Latin-American peoples.

Hammering again on the theme of Soviet–Thai "collusion," the VPT repeated its claim on July 8, 1969, that, according to the Thai

Foreign Minister, the Russians had indicated that they would provide support to Thailand and had given assurance that communist threats against Thailand would be prevented if only Thailand gave up its involvement in the Vietnam War. In effect, Peking was suggesting that Moscow was ready to abandon support for local communists if the price was right while Peking would do no such thing, thus also linking animosity toward the Soviet Union with opposition to the United States. To the VPT and Peking, the Soviet Union was now internally totally capitalist in outlook; externally it had become "social-imperialist."

From the Thai view of PRC–Thai relations during the first six months of 1969 there appeared to be slightly less rigidity *on the surface*—although one should be careful in interpreting certain Thai pronouncements. One such was Dr. Thanat's statement in March 1969,[17] repeating what he had said on previous occasions: that Thailand was ready to negotiate with communist countries—referring here to both the PRC and North Vietnam—"provided they are ready and sincere enough to seek peace." He added, "We will stick to morals and interests of the country." Thai policy should be flexible, according to Thanat, in order to adapt to changes in the world situation, and it should try to promote regional cooperation. However, "there will be *no neutrality* [italics added] in our policy," which can be taken as a reaffirmation of Thailand's alignment on the side of the United States.

On March 19, 1969, Dr. Thanat elaborated his position in an address to an American Management Association Seminar.[18] He called on all non-communist nations in Southeast Asia to close ranks so as to induce Communist China "to come out" and "work with us." If cooperation among the countries in the region was not forthcoming, on the other hand, Peking would remain a threat to their survival. As for the Soviet Union, he noted that it had sent naval detachments into the Indian Ocean, promoted contact with India, Indonesia, and Burma, and was ready to establish diplomatic relations with Singapore, Malaysia, and the Philippines. "These are not signs of disengagement by the USSR," remarked the Foreign Minister. Finally, regarding U.S. military presence in his own country, his position was that Thailand would never become a second Vietnam because "we are not going to let that happen." The fifty thousand U. S. troops in Thailand were there for the Vietnam War, while Thailand was fighting communist subversion on its own. "We do not look to American youth to risk their lives for the Thais," said Thanat. This statement was clearly meant for the larger American audience and the U. S. Congress, and not just for the group gathered in Bangkok.

The Thai Foreign Minister expanded on his views on Communist China in an interview given to U. S. and Australian journalists two days later.[19] He said that Thailand was not anti-Chinese, yet Marshall Chen I had reportedly said that China wanted to launch guerrilla warfare against Thailand. Thanat told the journalists that he would like to know whether the Chinese Foreign Minister had been quoted correctly, and if so, what had motivated Chen and what were the possibilities for coexistence. Thanat noted that he had last talked with Marshall Chen in Jakarta during the celebrations of the tenth anniversary of the Bandung Conference in 1965. He had not talked with the Chinese since then, nor had China made many contacts with foreign countries since the 1965 meeting.

As far as Thanat was concerned, he was making an offer to Peking through this interview. In his words, "so *in making this offer* [italics added] we hope that Peking may be interested in having further contacts with the outside world, which seemed to have disappeared." Revealing his concern about the firmness of U. S. commitments to Thailand, he added, "At present, while I am talking, the Symington Committee is reviewing U. S. commitments in regard to Thailand and Asia and we here, to be frank and honest, are reviewing our commitments to the outside world. We want to make it very plain that the national interest of Thailand and the regional interest of Southeast Asia are predominant. Thus an overture is made to Peking to the effect that Thailand is ready to sit down and talk with the Chinese if they are willing."

Thailand's readiness to enter into discussion with Peking was again stressed by Dr. Thanat in addressing the Thai Parliament on March 25, 1969.[20] "At present," he said, "we are restricted to fighting communist subversion within our own country. In demonstrating our wish for peace, we have a diplomatic weapon for an offensive." Should talks produce peace and stability, the money going into communist suppression operations could be used for schools and hospitals. On the other hand, the proposed talks with Peking would not mean any relaxation in the fight against communist terrorists within the country. Referring broadly to criticisms of Thailand in the U. S. Congress and press, he added: "Enemies have become the best of friends, allies the worst of enemies." Partly in his own defense against critics, Thanat thus stated his position that Thailand had to make reassessments of its foreign policy which would be based on safeguarding Thai independence.

The official Thai position was further clarified by the Thai Prime Minister in answer to a question in Parliament on the same day. According to Thanom, Thailand's offer to negotiate with Peking was based on the supposition that the latter would first change its aggressive policy.[21]

This initial Thai offer apparently was not accepted or even seriously considered by Peking, probably because of preoccupation with the Soviet threat and internal struggle following the Ninth Congress.

By mid-year, according to the *Bangkok World*,[22] Dr. Thanat had to report that there was no word from Peking in response to his overtures—"not even insults or abuse." Still smarting under U. S. press criticism, he remarked that the communists were usually very free with insults, even matching the western press in this respect. However, no word had been received from Peking. He expressed his doubt about the feasibility of a Soviet-led collective security arrangement in Asia that would include non-communist nations. He had received no details about the proposed security pact which, however, seemed to him to indicate the Soviet Union's thinking in terms of blocs and force. He added that Thailand would "watch with interest" development of the common security concept *if it is designed to contain Communist China*. He thought that military alliances would not have much appeal to Thailand under prevailing circumstances. Thailand would prefer to depend more on its wits than on the charity of outside support.[23]

The Foreign Minister's disappointment with Peking was intensified by the latter's military and para-military activities. A *Bangkok Post* report on July 8, 1969, attributed to a statement by Deputy Prime Minister Praphat Charusathian, stated that Chinese and North Vietnamese Communists were now directly threatening Thailand through a strategic road and a military post in Laos. The road was built by the Chinese from Cheli in South China through Phong Saly in northern Laos to a point only about three hours by motor vehicle from the border of Thailand. The post referred to was at Muong Soui, and its occupation by the communists would entail their control of the left bank of the Mekong River in northern Laos. This post stands on the invasion routes leading to Chiang Rai and Nan Uptaradit in Thailand.

Thanat's remarks concerning the Soviet Union were not unnoticed by Peking. On July 13, 1969, the VPT radio accused the Thai Foreign Minister of making excuses for the Soviet Union in the latter's expansion into the Mediterranean and the Indian Ocean, including the alleged establishment of a Soviet nuclear submarine base in Indian territorial waters "only about 10 kilometers from Thailand." The VPT said that Thanat had concurred in the Soviet revisionists' scheme to encircle the People's Republic of China. Also, Soviet offers of economic and military aid to India had helped strengthen Indian forces so that they could wage war against the PRC and had made the Soviet Union a very popular and respectable country in its relations with India.

According to the VPT, Thanat thought that expansion by Soviet revisionists into the Indian Ocean to carry out aggression against the PRC would benefit the Asian people. He reportedly believed that an agreement had been reached between U. S. imperialists and Soviet revisionists on some scheme of joint aggression against the PRC and on their plans to redivide the world. Peking's position on Thailand and on U.S.–Soviet "conspiracy" to maintain world hegemony—which was supposedly abetted in some way by Thailand—apparently had remained unchanged up to the time of President Nixon's Guam speech.

Mid-1969 to Spring 1971. There was relatively little movement in the position of both sides during the next two years. Through the NCNA and the clandestine VPT, Peking continued to call upon the "Thai people" to expand their struggle against the Thai government which it denounced in the name of the "people of Thailand" for having turned over Thai territory to the "U. S. imperialists" as a military base in the Vietnam War. This was the official Peking and Thai communist attitude as late as mid-February 1971.[24] Both Peking and the VPT extolled the virtue of a "people's war," pointing to Vietcong victories as testimony to the thesis that "the people of a small country can certainly defeat aggression by a big country, *if only they dare to rise in struggle, dare to take up arms* [italics added] and grasp in their own hands the destiny of their country."[25] The "total defeat of the U. S. aggressors" was loudly echoed for Thai listeners by the VPT when the same theme was announced by Chou En-lai during the visit of his party to Hanoi on March 3–8, 1971.

While there was little real concern by the Thai government in the beginning of 1971 about Peking's direct armed intervention as a result of increased U. S. and South Vietnamese activities in southeastern Laos since the site of such action was still about one thousand kilometers away from the Chinese border,[26] Thai officials were careful to minimize Thailand's role in allied military actions. Thai troops on alert on the Thai-Laotian border were said to have remained strictly on the Thai side.[27] Even on the question of trade with China, restrictions of which were being relaxed by the United States, official Thai comment on U. S. policy in mid-April 1971 was: "We must wait and see."[28] Thailand was not automatically to follow in the footsteps of the United States by permitting open trade with mainland China. Dealing with a communist country was still prohibited by law.

Spring 1971 to October 1971.   The plot of U. S.–Peking rapprochement began to thicken, and one can detect a visible difference in the degree of movement between the Thai and the Communist Chinese sides.[29] An apparent readiness for discussion on the part of Peking was accompanied by continued denunciations of the Thai government and military activities; on the Thai side, this was met by clear evidence of divided counsel. Some Thai officials thought that Peking's faint signals of a more relaxed attitude toward Thailand should be taken at face value and welcomed with warmth and relief. Others wanted Peking to cease its support of insurgency in Thailand before any further response was made by Bangkok. Among the pessimists, some even doubted that there had been meaningful signals from Peking.

Speaking to newsmen at the Don Muang Airport upon his return from Europe in May 1971, Foreign Minister Thanat Khoman announced that Peking had used a third country to contact Thailand.[30]

"Peking is interested in our opinions and what is happening here," he reported. Only a few days later, in an exclusive interview reported in the *Bangkok Post,* he was said to be visibly optimistic.[31] "Our differences have narrowed. Peking leaders have begun to understand us. It may well lead to a real dialogue." As the *Post* reported, Thanat then referred to Communist China for the first time as the "People's Republic of China."[32]

While Thanat was hopeful about a dialogue with Peking, the Thai communists and Peking itself did not let up their attack on the Thai government; nor did insurgent activities and the government's suppression operations slacken. On April 27, 1971, Bunchana Atthakor, Economic Affairs Minister, told the *Bangkok Post* that Peking had not stopped its radio attacks against Thailand and was supporting insurgency in the country. The Peking-sponsored VPT continued to address the Thai government as the "Thanom–Praphat clique" that had "sold out [our] independence to U. S. imperialism,"[33] and to report "brilliant victories" of terrorist operations.[34]

According to General Praphat Charusathian, Deputy Premier and Interior Minister, most of the weapons used by insurgents were supplied from abroad through remote border areas, some brought into Thailand by smugglers, others by "foreign countries."[35] Pote Sarasin, Minister of National Development and another Deputy Prime Minister, was more direct. Speaking to the *Bangkok Post,* he noted, "If Red China stops supplying weapons to communist terrorists in the country as well as . . . its propaganda against us, then relations could be initiated."[36] On May 24 the *Post* was to report that a "go-slow" policy was ordered by Prime Minister Thanom on approaches to Communist China until Peking's support of insurgency in Thailand had ceased. Even Dr. Thanat was emphatic about not allowing Peking to set up an embassy in Thailand. However, he "would like to have state-to-state contact with Peking instead of allowing the Chinese Communists to maintain their contacts with the insurgents."[37]

At the same time, the government decided against opening trade with the PRC. Fear was expressed in some quarters that even a trade mission from Peking and trade contacts, not to mention a Chinese Communist Embassy in Bangkok, could increase the chance of subversion. Yet the official position on trade was equivocal. Like "good businessmen" of most countries, even General Praphat was not against selling Thai goods to Communist China. The anti-communist law, he was reported to say, only prohibited communist activities; it did not prohibit sale of goods to communist countries.[38] Among the ideas advanced by Thai businessmen was indirect trading through Hong Kong by firms established especially for this purpose under government licensing, as distinct from firms trading with Taiwan.[39] The maintenance of bilateral balance in trading was also advocated.

Shortly before Mr. Nixon's announcement on July 15, 1971, of his planned visit to Peking, Prime Minister Thanom again voiced Thailand's fear of Peking's support for Thai insurgents. He was concerned about increased infiltration into Thai territory by communist terrorists from Laos and about the Communist Chinese-built road from Yunnan to Pak Ben and the Mekong River in Thailand.[40] This explains his cool reception of the Malaysian proposal that the United States, the Soviet Union, and Communist China guarantee the neutrality of Southeast Asia.[41] Premier Thanom informed his Malaysian counterpart that Thailand could not be neutral because "Communist China is carrying out a war of insurgency against our country."[42]

In an interview on July 14, Thai Deputy Foreign Minister Sa-Nga Kittikachorn told a local newsman that Thailand might have to "bend with the mounting trend to be more friendly with Communist China."[43] Yet when Thai officials learned the next day of the U.S. announcement, which took them by surprise, many advised caution. The same General Sa-Nga noted that as a small country Thailand could only be a spectator of world events. "We must first and foremost take care of our own interests."[44] He added, "we should consider the problem of maintaining the freedom of the Chinese Nationalists and the Taiwanese people on Taiwan in the context of world peace." The last reference indicated Thailand's opposition to the admission of Peking into the UN and Thai support for the Republic of China in the looming fight on the issue of Chinese representation in the UN General Assembly.[45]

In spite of an occasional voice advocating faster rapprochement with Peking,[46] the dominant general opinion, both in the government and among opposition politicians, was still to go slow. The U.S. announcement was officially welcomed as a step toward relaxation of tension, but some criticisms were quite outspoken. Thep Chotinuchit, leader of the Economist United Front Party and once jailed on

charges of engaging in communist activities because he had advocated trade with Peking, described President Nixon's proposed visit
in highly unflattering terms.[47] Speaking from a different vantage
point, Lt. General Saiyud Kerdphol, Director of the Communist Suppression Operations Command (CSOC), regarded the new U.S. policy
as a "tacit admission of defeat in the Indochina war."[48] The real issue
for Thailand, however, was plainly described by a Thai columnist as
follows: "the expected harmony between the two countries [i.e., the
United States and Communist China] does not mean that such Southeast Asian countries as Vietnam, Laos, Thailand and the Malayan
Peninsula will be safe, since Communist China is pursuing a perma-
nent policy of 'war of liberation' and 'world liberation.' The United
States is expected to withdraw its troops and use diplomacy. But this
will not stop Red China's desires. Then Southeast Asia will become
a public park for the Communist Chinese to roam around in with no
resistance."[49]

According to Lt. General Saiyud, "terrorists"—i.e., communist
insurgents—were still "alarmingly active" as late as September 1971,
when the Chinese representation issue was before the United Nations.[50] Terrorist attacks in Phitsanulok, Loei, and Phetchabun provinces were reported earlier by the clandestine VPT.[51] In the same
areas as well as in Nan, Prae, and Uttaradit provinces, harassment of
construction workers was rampant on the strategic Lomsak–Chumpoe
or east–west highway being built by Thailand in the northeast as a
countermeasure against the increase in infiltration capability by communists as a result of the Chinese-built road on the Thai-Laotian
border.[52] There were also increased military activities on the Thai-
Malaysian border.

These communist activities supplied some of the reasons for concern expressed by Thai authorities; they helped explain why Thailand
favored dual Chinese representation in the United Nations, but was
unwilling to recognize Peking diplomatically. As stated by Foreign
Minister Thanat more than a month before the crucial vote, Thailand's position on the Albanian-sponsored resolution to seat Peking
in the United Nations in place of the Chinese Nationalists was in
support of Nationalist China. It was not to oppose Peking's member-
ship if the latter should receive sufficient votes.[53] On September 10,
1971, the Thai National Security Council adopted a resolution to vote
for the admission of Communist China into the United Nations pro-

vided that a UN seat be reserved for the Chinese Nationalists.[54] The planned affirmative vote in favor of Peking's admission was intended to persuade Peking to drop its hostility toward Thailand after its entry into the United Nations. On September 15 Thailand's acting Foreign Minister further stated that the intended vote for Peking would not mean "that we will follow up with either trade or diplomatic relations."[55] Further clarification on the prospects for open Thai–Peking trade followed on September 20 when Bunchana Atthakor, Minister of Economic Affairs, said that Thailand should trade with Communist China only after the establishment of diplomatic relations and that he saw no immediate benefits to be gained from such trade.[56] Such relations might be established, however, two to three years after Peking's admission into the United Nations.[57]

While the Thai government was undergoing this painful reexamination of its China policy, it was subjected to more hostility from Peking and the clandestine Voice of the People of Thailand. Thanom was described as "the illegitimate prime minister" who had sold out "tens of thousands of Thais" as mercenaries.[58] The VPT promised to wage relentless struggle to the finish against the government. By October, the road from Laos being constructed by Chinese troops and engineers had reached a point only thirty-eight kilometers from the Mekong River on the Thai border.[59] A top communist cadre training school was reportedly functioning in Nakhorn Phanom.[60]

These were the prevailing circumstances when the U. S. motion for dual representation—which Thailand had finally agreed to co-sponsor—was defeated. Apparently the Thai authorities had not expected the result to be "so disastrous," as General Sa-Nga put it, "for the U. S."[61] Significantly, unlike other co-sponsors of the defeated resolution, Thailand then abstained on the Albanian resolution to admit Peking and expel Taiwan. This was an attempt to minimize damage, and was apparently in accordance with the position expressed earlier by Thanat.

Recrimination after the UN defeat was to be expected. Seni Pramoj, leader of the major opposition Democrat Party, repeated his frequent call upon the Thanom government to reconsider its attitude toward Peking.[62] The leader of the People's Party, Liang Chaiyakarn, who favored admission of Peking but was against expulsion of Taiwan, said that the government would have to resign before Thailand's policy toward Peking could be adjusted.[63] Phaitu Khruakaeo, **leader** of the pro-Peking Democratic Front Party, urged that both Field Marshall Thanom and Dr. Thanat should now resign as a minimum gesture of policy adjustment,[64] and that trade with Peking and diplomatic recognition should be instituted without delay. The same policy change was advocated by Thep Chotinuchit of the Economist–United Front Party who, however, suggested that the government should resign en masse.[65] Furthermore, Thep thought that "American bases should be moved out as a gesture of relaxation of tension with Peking." Those who advocated an immediate about-face in Thailand's attitude toward China felt that a new policy would evoke a favorable Chinese response in the form of lessened insurgency. Implicitly, they seemed to accept the government's thesis that the insurgents were supported by Peking and under the latter's orders or direct influence. Even Seni, who wanted to watch Peking's attitude, hoped that a change might be forthcoming; he cited the cancellation of the usual military parade on October 1, the PRC's national day, as a possible sign.[66]

The immediate communist response to the UN vote was quick in coming. A VPT broadcast in Thai on October 29 called the outcome of the UN contest "a shameful defeat for U. S. imperialism and its lackeys," including among the latter the Thanom–Praphat clique. This defeat was to "end the influential role played by U. S. imperialism" in the United Nations, and showed the international situation to be "developing in a direction favorable for the people's revolution." It was an admission that "major international issues could not be solved without PRC participation." In the judgment of the VPT, however, "U. S. imperialism's aggressive nature [had] never changed." As for the Thai government, it "had to suffer ignominy along with its U. S. masters." Among its mistaken ways were "adopting a policy hostile to the PRC following the United States; . . . cherishing the Chiang Kai-shek clique . . . ; barring the Thai people from freely making contacts with Chinese people."

In the face of the storm of criticism and communist hostility, the government's official policy was to continue to watch for any possible change in Peking's policy toward Thailand. There would be no change in its position on trade, and no official contact with Peking would be contemplated. Diplomatic relations with Taiwan would be maintained.[67] General Sa-Nga went so far as to announce that he would resign if the government were to decide on establishing diplomatic relations with Communist China.[68] While the government and its opponents might differ on their respective evaluations of Peking's intentions, they seemed to agree that Thailand made a mistake in identifying itself with the U. S. position. As Seni put it, "Many countries which earlier adopted an anti-communist policy with the support of the United States have become disillusioned and no longer had any confidence in the American government in view of America's troop withdrawal from various parts of the world and its changeable policy."[69]

November 1971 to October 1973. The division of opinion continued on how long Thailand should or could "wait and see." The day after the Prime Minister's press interview on November 1, a meeting was held by the Thai National Security Council to consider the Communist China problem. An article by Banyat Tasaneeyavig reported in the *Bangkok Post* of November 4 that the Council then decided to remove the ban on trade with Peking,[70] to relax existing anti-communist laws, and to permit visits to Peking by sport and non-political missions. The Ministry of Economic Affairs reportedly was instructed to design controls for the regulation of trade with Peking. The Council also was said to have ruled against establishing diplomatic relations with Peking in the near future and against permitting political figures and others to visit the PRC as individuals.

At about the same time, Foreign Minister Thanat told the press that Thai policy toward Peking would be kept in step with that of other countries in the region.[71] In his words, "We can trade with China anytime. We can scrap Order No. 53 of the Revolutionary Party's Announcement anytime." Several days later Dr. Thanat announced that he had received cabinet approval to begin a dialogue with Peking, apparently at the ambassadorial level.[72] Even the Prime Minister, who had maintained a firm line, was quoted as saying, "The softening of the government attitude toward mainland China is aimed at paving the way for further relations with that country after it has been admitted to the United Nations."[73]

Deputy Prime Minister General Praphat opposed this movement toward a more rapid rapprochement with Peking and reminded Dr. Thanat that Chen I's proclaimed "war of national liberation" against

Thailand had not yet been renounced.[74] He charged that the Chinese Communists were still supporting insurgents in Thailand and that advocates of immediate diplomatic recognition of Peking were either panicky or ignorant.

Without going into details of Thai domestic politics, one can state with some confidence that the failure of Thailand's policy of open adherence to U. S. strategy in the United Nations in October 1971 and the resultant uncertainty about internal security and the government's ability to deal with it contributed significantly to Field Marshall Thanom's decision to establish a National Executive Council (NEC) in place of the government he had headed. This self-administered "coup" took place on November 17, 1971, and the new government, still under Thanom and Praphat but without the open interference of opposition politicians, was to continue in power for nearly two years. Foreign Minister Thanat, then among the advocates of a faster approach to Peking, was dropped from the inner circles after the coup although foreign policy differences were not necessarily the only reason.

Establishment of the new political framework under the same personal political leadership did not alter communist perception of Thailand's official policy. The clandestine VPT, describing the NEC heads as the "traitorous, piratic, fascist, dictatorial Thanom–Praphat clique,"[75] noted Marshall Thanom's interview with *The New York Times* in which he affirmed that the NEC would maintain the same relations with the United States, SEATO, Japan, and Taiwan as before.[76] To quote the VPT, "The clique will continue to pursue its traitorous policy in service of U. S. aggression and exploitation." Throughout November and December 1971 attacks were reported on government positions in the northeast in Ubon Ratchathani.[77] In the north, government sources spoke of a stepped-up flow of arms from Communist China[78] and increasingly serious insurgency in Chiang Rai, Nan, and Loei provinces.[79] While intensified insurgency and the government's response to it were by no means solely a function of Peking's aid to the guerrillas, both Peking and the Thai government apparently saw each other in the role of opponents and considered it appropriate to regard each other in this light.

If 1972 was a year of reconciliation between Peking and Washington, it brought Thailand more turmoil. According to Puang Suwan-

narath, Under Secretary for the Interior, communist Vietnamese and
Laotian guerrillas joined Meo and Thai insurgents in attacks on
government camps and road construction workers.[80] The *Bangkok
Post* of January 5, 1972, reported the guerrillas to be active militarily
in the north and the northeast, with political headquarters in parts
of Sakon Nakhon, Kalasin, Nakhorn Phanom, and northern Ubon.
The U. S. airbase at Utapao was attacked for the first time in early
January, according to one report.[81] Widespread military action in
various parts of the country, including the north, the northeast, and
the south, was reported by the communists themselves.[82] The number
of PRC road workers on the "infiltration route" from China to Pak
Ben, twenty-four kilometers from the Thai-Laotian border, was
reported in February to have risen to five thousand.[83]

    Increased insurgent activities did not seem to be solely a response
to greater government counter-insurgency efforts.[84] In its New Year
message, the VPT spoke in typical Maoist style:

> The revolutionary strength of the people all over the world has
> vigorously expanded and scored brilliant victories. The position
> of U. S. imperialism, Soviet social imperialism, the reactionary
> Thanom–Praphat clique, and the reactionaries in other countries
> has deteriorated.... The people's armed forces have sapped the
> strength of the U. S.–Thanom clique,... [adopted] tactics of a
> war of systematic destruction,... seized a greater quantity of
> weapons and equipment from the enemy to arm themselves,...
> [and] constantly expanded the battlefield and won over a large
> number of the masses.... On the political plane the clique has
> become extremely isolated.[85]

The Maoist "textbook" language was consistent with the words
Peking chose to use through NCNA. Quoting the VPT, NCNA stated
on February 2, 1972: "While withdrawing some of its troops from
South Vietnam, the U.S. at the same time stepped-up implementing
the Nixon Doctrine of fighting the Vietnamese with Vietnamese and
Asians with Asians." Again, the U. S. "must stop using Thailand as a
base for aggression against Indochinese countries." Shortly before
Mr. Nixon's visit to Peking, NCNA quoted the VPT: "U. S. imperialism is absolutely unwilling to leave Thailand, but... [will] make use

of this country as a military base for aggression in Indochina and this region."[86]

Developments during 1972 were most illuminating on the perilous process of change in perception. A change in attitude on the part of another country could be perceived when none has taken place, just as an actual change on the part of one country may be unobserved by another. This complication is further compounded by the communist practice—increasingly accepted and sometimes even openly emulated by the West—of exhibiting friendliness toward another country at the official level while simultaneously plotting the overthrow of its government.

This "two-level" relationship as practiced by Peking was graphically illustrated in its dealings with Thailand during 1972. On the one hand, military operations by both the government and the insurgents continued through the year, hardly affected either before or afterwards by President Nixon's Peking visit. On the other hand, signals emanating from Peking in the summer of that year were read by Thai authorities as a possible softening of the PRC's attitude toward Thailand. At times they were avidly grasped as the long-awaited diplomatic breakthrough, but at other times they were observed hesitantly and with apparent trepidation. The year ended with a stand-off. A new Thai–PRC relationship died aborning because, in the final analysis, the then Thai government was not prepared to accept Peking's two-level approach: official "friendship" accompanied by unofficial support of subversion and revolution.

A stepped-up military campaign by the government started at the end of January 1972. Operation Phu Kwang, a large joint effort by the army and the air force, was aimed at insurgents in the mountainous Phitsanulok–Loei–Phetchabun border area. A National Executive Council report on March 17—shortly after Mr. Nixon's return from Peking—claimed complete government victory in the Phu Longkha mountain range.[87] In April, the government further claimed "good results" in its communist suppression campaign, "particularly along the southern border."[88] No less a person than Marshall Thanom spoke of documentary evidence pointing to contacts between "terrorists" and "Chinese bandits" in the Thai-Malaysian border areas in Nakhon Si Thammarat, Surat Thani, and Phattalung. In order to combat insurgency in the south, a joint Thai-Malaysian Border Command was set up. Under this arrangement, Malaysian troops would serve under Thai command in the Waeng district of Narathiwat Province and the Betong district of Yala Province, while Thai troops would serve under Malaysian command when operating on the Malaysian side.[89] Official reports of widespread operations in north, northeast, south, and central Thailand continued into the summer.[90]

On August 10, a general round-up of communist suspects took place in Bangkok and other cities in an attempt to forestall organized urban uprisings coordinating with insurgent operations in the country. Simultaneously, under the BE (Buddhist Era) 2495 (i.e., 1952) Anti-communist Act and the 1969 Amendment, the power of detention was extended on suspects held for interrogation in cases involving national security and public order. Such suspects could now be held without trial for an indefinite period.[91] One source gave the total number of arrests during the round-up as ninety-eight; thirty-three persons in the Bangkok metropolitan area and sixty-five in the provinces.[92] Only two to three percent of those arrested were said to be Thai; according to the police, the overwhelming majority was Chinese.[93]

To intensify the drive against potential urban guerrillas, Lt. General Saiyud announced on August 18, 1972, that rewards of up to ten thousand baht would be offered for the death or capture of top communists whose names appeared on a list soon to be issued. The idea of offering bounty—one thousand baht for any insurgent killed in his jungle uniform—was proposed by Major General Suwan Intulak, Governor of Phattalung Province.[94] Such extreme measures and the mass arrests clearly reflected both the perception by the authorities of intensified threat and, perhaps, their hope that firmer control over the domestic insurgency problem would enable the government to deal more effectively with Peking—and, incidentally, with North Vietnam—thus paving the way for a rapprochement on the state-to-state level.

As one might expect in such operations, however, communist guerrillas moved back to the mountainous area following the withdrawal of government forces in Operation Phu Kwang.[95] There followed occasional reports of reduced guerrilla activities,[96] but it was difficult to determine the relative importance of reasons for the reduction—the effectiveness of government efforts, the rainy season, etc. The U. S. airbases at Udon and Ubon were attacked in early October.[97] With the arrival of the dry season in December, the CSOC reported that communist operations had again increased.[98] General Praphat Charusathian announced on November 24, through the NEC press center, that the Chinese-built road toward the Thai border had reached the Mekong River and that a bridge was now under construction.[99]

At no time during this period did the communist insurgents seem really to have lessened their effort. In mid-March 1972, they claimed to have "wiped out over 800 enemy troops, nearly half the total number . . . wiped out in 1971."[100] Claiming "vigorous attacks" against government forces "in the North, Northeast, South, and Central parts of Thailand," they boasted of having "kindled the raging flame of people's war," an aphorism again characteristically Maoist.[101] The next month, Peking's NCNA credited the VPT with reports of "fresh victories" in the Phitsanulok, Loei, and Phetchabun area.[102] An article broadcast by the VPT and relayed by NCNA on May 18 claimed that the insurgents had "wiped out over 830 men . . . from January to April." Claims of successful encounters with government forces were issued from time to time without any real interruption.[103] Both U. S. and Thai government forces were accused by VPT on September 5 of having employed chemical and biological warfare in destroying food supply in Phitsanulak, Loei, and Phetchabun.

Notably, however, NCNA now spoke of "the spirit of self-reliance" displayed by the Communist Party of Thailand in the past seven years (1965–72) of revolutionary warfare.[104] The Central Committee of the Thai Communist Party was more explicit. In an editorial comment on the December 1, 1972, statement of the Central Committee commemorating the Party's 30th anniversary, the VPT explained:

> By employing peaceful means, the revolutionaries only become the victims of arbitrary arrests and executions by the reactionaries. . . . The revolution can be achieved only when it is carried out by the peasants waging the people's war, building up base areas upcountry, surrounding towns with villages and eventually seizing the towns. The armed struggle in the rural areas is, therefore, a major struggle coordinated with other forms of struggle. *The struggle in urban areas must support the armed struggle*

being carried on in rural areas. This is the way to make the revo-
lution self-reliant and keep it always on the road to success [italics
added].[105]

These remarks explained the previously mentioned governmental
concern about urban insurgency, because the ideological outlook
revealed by the communist insurgents did not permit political com-
promise. *Prima facie,* it would be ideologically inconsistent for the
communists to abandon open insurgency either on their own or at
the behest of Peking. How much support, internal or external, the
hard core of insurgents can receive at any time is a different matter.
The latter depends upon the effectiveness of government policy—not
just upon counter-insurgency measures—as well as upon the tactical
moves of Peking.

Efforts were made by Peking and Thailand to develop official
relations at a different level, however, in spite of the insurgency and
counter-insurgency operations during this period. Receipt of the first
clear signal from Peking was announced in Bangkok about two
months after the Nixon visit to mainland China and following com-
pletion of the first phases of the Phu Kwang counter-insurgency
operations. It took the form of an invitation by the executive committee of the Asian Table Tennis Union to the Table Tennis Association of Thailand for Thai participation in a ping-pong match in
Peking in September 1972.[106] More than two months were to pass
before General Praphat Charusathian, Deputy Director of the NEC,
announced that a Thai team would be permitted to participate in
the games.[107] According to General Praphat, an invitation would also
be extended to a PRC team in reciprocity. Appointed to accompany
the team as advisor was the deputy chief of the Directorate of
Finance, Economic Affairs and Industry of the NEC, Prasit Kan-
chanawat, Board Chairman of a Bangkok bank, who happened to be
a confidant of General Praphat.[108] The manager of the Thai team was
Police Lt. General Chumpon Lohachala, incumbent commissioner of
the Central Investigation Bureau of the Police Department.

The functions of these non-players was a matter of considerable—
and customary—equivocation. General Chumpon told the press that,
while in Peking, he would make himself available for contacts with
Thai exiles. "If any Thai in China wants to see me, I shall be glad to

meet him."[109] According to a Bangkok radio report on August 4, 1972, Marshall Thanom claimed that he had not given any policy guidance to the Thai delegation and that there would not be any "talks" with the Chinese. A report in *The Nation,* however, claimed that Thanom expected Prasit to "discuss with high-ranking Chinese officials about the possibility of trade."[110] General Praphat agreed that the possibility of establishing trade relations with China existed; however, he noted that he was as yet unaware of Peking's conditions for trade,[111] apparently referring to Thailand's relationship with Taiwan. Three days after this interview, General Praphat told reporters that Prasit, who speaks Chinese, would "only be advising the Thai team on Chinese language and culture."[112] In a similar reversal, General Chumpon, leader of the Thai team, told the press that it would not be necessary for Thailand to invite a PRC team to take part in any tournament, and "[that] it [was] not our duty."[113]

In the course of these verbal gymnastics—which, deliberately designed or not, had the effect of creating uncertainty about Thailand's ultimate attitude in Peking's eyes and of paying heed to divergent domestic opinions—a cable came from the Chinese Table Tennis Association inviting the Thai team to stay on after the tournament as its guest. This was interpreted in Bangkok as a "gesture of friendship."[114] The *Bangkok Post* claimed that Mr. Prasit was preparing for informal talks in Peking on a variety of major issues, including "alleged Peking support for communist insurgency in Thailand, peaceful coexistence, Thai exiles in China, Thais of Chinese descent in China, dual nationality for persons born in Thailand of Chinese parents, the Taiwan problem, trade, people-to-people contacts, possible development of future relations, [and] Chinese representation in the ECAFE headquarters in Bangkok."[115] This and a similar report by *The Nation* on the same day were promptly denied by Prasit as "baseless" and misleading.[116]

Prasit met with Chou En-lai in Peking as the former apparently had hoped. According to the Bangkok radio, Prasit told newsmen upon his return from Peking "that the PRC premier understood and sympathized with various problems of Thailand and was ready to establish contacts."[117] He reported that Peking was willing to trade with Thailand. On the question of overseas Chinese, he said that the PRC thought that the latter should obey the laws of their country of residence and act as good citizens. Amidst feelings of confidence that Peking had changed its stance more than a little, nevertheless there was no real assurance that it would not continue its support of Thai insurgents. All that Prasit could secure from Chou was a statement that "China would not interfere with the domestic affairs of other countries but would encourage the people to fight for freedom."[118] There could hardly be a clearer expression of the PRC's two-level approach.

Very soon after the Prasit visit to Peking, the PRC, through the Thai trade commission in Hong Kong, officially invited a Thai trade delegation to visit the Canton Trade Fair opening on October 15, 1972.[119] This was hailed in Bangkok as another forward step by Peking.[120] Additional steps were expected when, once again, the question of PRC support for insurgents in Thailand came to the fore. The occasion was the appearance of a Chinese-made 130-mm artillery shell at the Mekong border, simultaneously with a reported increase in Chinese- and North Vietnamese-supported insurgent activities in different parts of Thailand.[121] As a result, the rapprochement between Bangkok and Peking was cut short. Little more would develop under the Thanom–Praphat government which fell in October 1973.

After Thanom–Praphat.   The principal questions facing Thailand in assessing the desirability of establishing relations with Peking and the nature of such relations are the following: First—apart from insurgency—there is concern about the possibility, however remote, of direct military incursion by North Vietnam or Communist China. Will the establishment of relations lessen this possibility? Will it reduce the capacity of insurgents in Thailand by creating a sense of being abandoned by Peking? Will it actually induce Peking to reduce Chinese support for these insurgents? Or will it have exactly the opposite effect? On the other hand, will refusal to establish such relations increase Peking's hostility and, therefore, its pressure on Thailand, including support of insurgency? Thailand's attitude toward Taiwan, which is regarded by Thai authorities as a counterweight to Peking among local Chinese in Thailand, partly hinges on the answers to these questions.

Since the questions cannot be answered with full assurance, how they should be evaluated is a function of Thailand's perception of the future. Not the least important is the degree of U. S. military presence in Thailand. United States willingness to use this presence to enforce the terms of the cease-fire in Vietnam, thereby keeping any direct major conflict away from Thailand, is another factor. Such concerns are based on Thailand's national interests and the availability of alternatives, and are essentially independent of the nature of the government.

To the Thai communists, short of a takeover by themselves, overthrow of the Thanom–Praphat government would not by itself remove the basic reasons for insurgency or for their need for Peking's support. The defeat of the Thanom–Praphat government by student revolt in October 1973 was initially hailed by the Peking government as a return of power to the people.[122] However, both the Thai communists and Peking soon changed their tune.[123] They felt that the revolution must be continued. The post-Thanom caretaker government under Prime Minister Sanya Dharmasakti resumed the probe of Peking's intentions which had begun under the previous regime by sending Air Marshall Dawee to Peking in his capacity as head of the Thai Olympic Committee.[124] Upon his return, Dawee reported that Chou En-lai had told him that the PRC was no longer supporting communist insurgents in Thailand, Laos, and other Southeast Asian countries.[125] Dr. Sanya, however, remained unconvinced.

Peking's credibility was still under question despite Chou's assurance and such economic baits as Peking's offer to sell crude oil to Thailand. Even if Peking called off its support of the insurgents for the moment, might it not change its mind again in the future? Thailand was not ready to abolish its anti-communist law and to take the Chinese communists at their word.

The 1973 change of government in Thailand and the formation of the second Sanya government in 1974 without Dawee or any other high military members were as yet insufficient to alter Thai policy. It remains to be seen, however, whether Malaysia's diplomatic recognition of Peking in June 1974, together with U. S. withdrawal of B–52 bombers from Thai bases, will finally overcome Thai reluctance to approach Peking, especially under the new Thai regime elected in January 1975.

PRC Relations with Malaysia and Singapore

Before the Cultural Revolution

Since the separation of Singapore to become a state independent of Malaysia did not take place until August 1965, Peking's relations with Malaysia encompassed its relations with Singapore during the greater part of the pre-Cultural Revolution period. The nature of this relationship, viewed from both sides, was unmistakably clear.

On April 29, 1965, the Central Committee of the Chinese Communist Party sent a congratulatory message to its counterpart in the Communist Party of Malaya on the occasion of the latter's 35th anniversary. Commending the Malayan Party for its long-standing role "at the forefront of the struggle against the imperialist rulers," the Chinese Communists reaffirmed their support for the Malay people's "just struggle."[126] A five-man delegation from Sarawak—a part of "North Kalimantan" in Peking's terminology—went to Communist China a month later at the invitation of the Chinese Committee for Afro-Asian Solidarity.[127] Representing the communist insurgents of Sarawak who desired separation from Malaysia, they were cordially greeted by Marshall Chen I, Peking's Foreign Minister and advocate of the violent overthrow of the government of Thailand, Malaysia's northern neighbor. It is not difficult to imagine what the visitors and the marshall discussed.

Four months later, as a sequel to the previous visit and following the separation of Singapore from Malaysia, the New China News Agency reported the arrival in Peking of an official delegation from the "North Kalimantan Unitary State." This time the visitors were received by Prime Minister Chou En-lai who expressed his admiration of their sustained effort to carry on revolution with inferior arms but superior organization and unity.[128] In these circumstances, it is not surprising that the Malaysian government should regard Peking's intentions as malevolent and as an attempt to break up the federal structure of Malaysia.

In an address delivered in Singapore on March 7, 1965, the then Malaysian Prime Minister, Tunku Abdul Rahman, accused Peking of having amassed 140 million Malaysian dollars in Hong Kong to pay for subversion in Malaysia. Peking's intent, according to the Tunku, was "to overthrow our country."[129] The Singapore branch of the Bank of China was suspected of being a conduit of funds for illegal activities. Malaysian authorities in June threatened to close the bank two months later.[130]

Malaysian concern about Peking seemed to involve the following factors. First, as the Tunku told the United Malay National Organization (UMNO) in May 1965, Peking was the one power whose aim was to dominate all Asia and to impose its communist ideology upon other Asians.[131] "This power lust regime," said the Prime Minister, "respects neither God nor man. It gives no freedom to those whom [it] rules. This is the sort of people [who] to my mind are the real imperialists."

Second, to quote the Tunku further, "When Malaysia was formed, what we had in mind was to build an invisible great wall stretching from the Siamese border to the sea which divides the Philippines and ourselves.... It was as a result of this that Indonesia started her confrontation. It is clear, therefore, that it was not Indonesia that took offense at the formation of Malaysia but the communists. Therefore, the whole confrontation by Indonesia is communist-inspired."[132] As perceived by the Malaysian government, the communist threat thus took the form of subversion, insurgency, and confrontation with Indonesia, all of which drew support and inspiration from Peking.

Third, speaking of those "communist sympathizers" among the Chinese in Malaysia, the Tunku noted that they wanted to turn Malaysia into a third China, contrary to the majority of Chinese residents who are realistic.[133] While defending the Malay position against Singapore's accusation that the Chinese were not fairly treated in Malaysia, the Malaysian Prime Minister thus expressed his concern that Peking might profit from internal conflict arising out of the racial issue.

Since the separation of Singapore from Malaysia had a strong racial undertone, it is important to note that immediately upon independence Singapore itself chose a middle ground on the sensitive PRC–Taiwan issue. Dr. Toh Chin Chye, the Deputy Prime Minister, while declaring Singapore's support for the admission of Peking to the United Nations, claimed that the interests of the people on Taiwan should also be considered. "On the other hand," said Toh, "you just cannot simply ignore the interests of the 10 million people in Formosa. This is a problem for the 10 million people in the country to decide. The issue is not a simple one of whether Formosa should be in the United Nations or not."[134]

On communal matters, the authorities of the newly-independent state now called for general recognition of Singapore's interdependence with Malaysia and stressed the need to establish a matter-of-fact relationship for mutual benefit.[135] Internally, the communists were treated as a disruptive group which skillfully and cynically exploited communal feelings and racial chauvinism. They were said to be backed by "outside sponsors" and "out to disrupt the consolidation of national identity."[136] Singapore, too, had no intention of becoming a "third China." The local Bank of China, however, was temporarily saved from an earlier closing threat as a result of Singapore's independence.[137]

After the Cultural Revolution

From 1969 to 1971

Initial Position of Malaysia. During 1969, when Peking was beginning to reassess its foreign policy and Washington's new China policy was still in the making, relations between Malaysia and Communist China closely resembled Thai–PRC relations during the same period. Peking-supported antigovernment statements and activities by insurgents—"terrorists" in official language—were met by equally clear official statements of policy and military activity on the Malaysian side. Official statements generally seemed to be milder than contemporary statements from Thailand, but there was clear recognition of the importance of counterinsurgency operations. Racial tension broke out in large-scale clashes on May 13, 1969. Preoccupation with the aftermath of the riot may have caused the government—*prima facie*—to be less vociferous in verbal retaliation against Peking and more mindful of fairly successful opposition activities by Malaysians after World War II when the country was still under British rule.

Toward the end of January 1969, Tun Razak, Deputy Prime Minister, stated that the country's consistent foreign policy was to be friends with those who were friendly toward Malaysia.[138] This was in reply to opposition suggestions that Malaysia should reorient its policy toward Communist China. Razak maintained that Peking should demonstrate its readiness to subscribe to peaceful coexistence and non-interference in the internal affairs of other countries. Malaysia had taken the same position in 1965 before its break with Singapore and before the Cultural Revolution interlude in China.

A little over a month later, according to a Singapore press report, Tunku Abdul Rahman declared that Malaysia was anxious to promote better relations with all countries and that it was even ready to establish diplomatic relations with the PRC if Peking "would allow us to lead our own way of life without undue interference."[139] In short, Malaysia was willing to take the initiative if Peking would only accept the independence of Malaysia and cease active efforts to undermine the latter's existing government. Tan Siewsin, then Finance Minister and the principal leader of Chinese origin who had the confidence of his Malay colleagues, spoke of the unity and solidarity of all Malaysians in spite of their diverse racial origins. At the General Assembly of the Malaysian-Chinese Association, which represented Chinese interests in an alliance with the United Malay Organization within the government, Tan said that good Malaysians should resist outside attempts to divide the country or to ignore the national identity of a unified Malaysia.[140]

The tentative early gestures toward Peking should be regarded as an integral part of Malaysia's domestic policy toward the Chinese elements in its population. The ethnically predominant Malay government probably did not wish to exacerbate racial disharmony by being hostile to Peking since some Chinese residents were sympathetic—or at least potentially friendly—toward the latter. The government was clearly hopeful that Peking might be persuaded to leave Malaysia alone. Unfortunately, these hopes—whether seriously entertained or not—were soon dashed by the large-scale race riot in May. The National Operations Council set up to deal with the emergency expressed its deep concern that communists and their agents deliberately worked to create disturbances and to disrupt racial harmony, especially in the rural areas.[141]

The Attitude of Peking and of Peking-supported Communists. Aside from active guerrilla operations both on the Thai-Malaysian border and in Sarawak, Peking's hostility toward Malaysia was verbally evident through its own mouthpiece, the New China News Agency, and through what purported to be "Malayan" media such as the clandestine radio, "Voice of Malayan Revolution" (VMR). Not infrequently NCNA would quote such a source in order to convey its own message without official responsibility. An important Peking objective seemed to be the creation of an atmosphere conducive to insurgency. In this regard Peking's policy toward Malaysia and the *modus operandi* were identical with those it employed in dealing with Thailand.

For instance, on January 18, 1969, NCNA reported that a New Year message of the Party Rayaat (The People's Party) was published in Singapore on that day stating that the revolutionary situation in the world had been "excellent" during the preceding year. This theme was repeated in the following month, the second time quoting the Singapore *Barisan* which had warmly acclaimed the "current excellent situation in world revolution."[142] According to NCNA, "the revolutionary people of Malaya" (i.e., in Peking's parlance, including Singapore) had been engaged in serious studies of Mao Tse-tung's thought and had learned several important lessons. These were that political power "grows out of the barrel of a gun," that all reactionaries are "paper tigers," and that it is only right for the people to rebel against their reactionary oppressors. On June 12 NCNA quoted the *People's Tribune,* identified as a Singapore paper, as saying that the "Rahman–Razak regime" was inciting racist sentiments in order to "prop up" its counterrevolutionary rule. Several days later, quoting the *Barisan,* NCNA stated that the Singapore publication had urged the Malayan people to rise against the Rahman government's "bloody oppression."[143] Peking was apparently trying to make mischief between Malaysia and Singapore over and above its general call for revolution.

As in the case of Thailand, Peking also attempted to link the governments of both Malaysia and Singapore to U. S. as well as Soviet schemes. Attacking the visit of a Soviet trade mission to the two countries, NCNA reported on April 4, 1969, that the *Barisan* had "sternly denounced the Soviet revisionist renegade clique for its intensified collusion with the Rahman–Lee ... puppet cliques—flunkeys of U. S. and British imperialism—and [for] its hideous betrayal of the interests of the Malayan people."

On November 8, 1969, a new clandestine radio began broadcasting from South China under the name of the "Voice of Malayan Revolution" (VMR).[144] Its adoption of the term "Malayan" was indicative of the official line of Peking which had never recognized the Federation of Malaysia—with or without Singapore—as an independent state. (Nor has it recognized the independence of Singapore.) The identity of its sponsorship was further revealed by the style of its writers, not to mention the contents of its message. For instance, to quote its first day of broadcasting: "Salute to the revolutionary people of all nationalities; salute to the heroic Malayan National Liberation Army. Long live the glorious Communist Party of Malaya. *Long live and a long life to Chairman Mao, the great teacher and the great leader of the world's people* [italics added]."[145]

The VMR claimed that its arrival on the scene broke the monopoly of its adversaries in radio broadcasting. Its objectives were to propagate the ideas of Marx, Lenin, and Mao Tse-tung; to eulogize the Malayan National Liberation Army; to "expose" and "crush" enemy plots and to prepare public opinion for the launching of an extensive "people's war" in Malaya. The purpose of this "people's war" was to defeat imperialism (meaning the United States and Britain), modern revisionism (meaning the Soviet Union), and all reactionaries at home (meaning the governments of Malaysia and Singapore), in order to establish a "people's republic" in all Malaya. Under this general guidance, a number of specific themes were subsequently developed by the VMR and were faithfully followed through all of 1970–71 and most of the time thereafter.

Guerrilla and Counter-insurgency Operations in 1969. Peking's verbal attacks and exhortations to revolution probably would not have seemed so threatening to Malaysian authorities if internal security had been stable. Unfortunately, deep-seated problems were revealed by NCNA reports, VMR broadcasts—the latter given wider circulation by NCNA—and announcements from Kuala Lumpur itself. The government frequently reported during 1969 discovery of deserted guerrilla camps on the Malaysian-Thai border, clashes between terrorists and Malaysian and Thai security forces, guerrilla crossings of the Malaysian-Thai border in both directions, use of artillery, jet fighters, and helicopters by Malaysian government forces, and cooperative efforts by Malaysia and Thailand to "mop up" the guerrillas.[146] In the same period, after the establishment of the VMR, frequent reports came from communist sources on successful ambushes, hit-and-run raids on police stations and government outposts, and claims of guerrilla success in eluding encircling government forces.[147] One estimate given by a Malaysian police spokesman in early April 1969 put the strength of the terrorists on the Thai border at nine hundred men.[148] According to this source, half of this force was made up by new recruits; if true, this would indicate a substantial growth at the beginning of this period. Ten thousand Malaysian and Thai security troops were reported by early September to be operating along the border against these insurgents.[149] The guerrillas were not rooted out, however, as subsequent developments clearly demonstrated.

In eastern Malaysia, both guerrilla and counterinsurgency operations were reported in 1969.[150] These occurred principally in parts of Sarawak bordering Kalimantan or Indonesian West Borneo. Terrorist attacks—mostly small-scale operations—were attributed to the North Borneo People's Army (Pasokan Raayat Kalimantan Ugara). To the extent that these operations resulted in government success, aid made available by the Indonesian government was said to be an important contributing factor.

More Communist Military and Non-military Attacks in 1970–71. The year 1970 was replete with the same kind of guerrilla attacks, counterinsurgency operations, VMR and NCNA exhortations to armed revolution, and verbal attacks against the existing authorities. An analysis of the themes adopted by the communists in attacking both the Malaysian and the Singapore governments, especially through the VMR, reveals a conscious effort to undermine economic development through foreign investment and to block the way of alternative foreign policy and defense options toward which both Malaysia and Singapore were groping. The principal themes were nationalism, including economic nationalism, and racial suspicion. Exploitation of issues in these areas was to become more and more important while armed revolution continued.

(a) Armed revolution: First, on the constant theme of armed revolution and the role of Peking, NCNA cited the 1970 New Year's Day editorial of the VMR and stated that the Malayan communists had "called on the people of various nationalities of Malaya to unite closely around the Communist Party of Malaya, ... using the countryside to encircle the cities and seizing political power through armed struggle." The VMR then claimed to have "shaken ... violently the reactionary rule of the Rahman-Razak clique and the Lee Kuan Yew clique" through tremendous communist victories.[151] Both NCNA and the VMR asserted that the latter's task was to propagate Mao Tse-tung's ideas and to create revolutionary opinion for further expansion of the continuing armed struggle.[152]

In a statement marking its 40th anniversary, the Malayan Communist Party acknowledged that it had made mistakes twice in the past, each time by actually or nearly giving up armed struggle. The last time it did this was under the influence of Liu Shao-ch'i and Khrushchev. The correct party line of persisting in armed struggle finally prevailed after 1961.[153] Finally, the VMR advocated a "new democratic revolution" for Malaysia and Singapore. Echoing Mao Tse-tung's May 1970 call for world revolution, the VMR promised to respond to the master's appeal for continuing struggle to defeat "U. S.-led imperialism and all its running dogs."[154]

Like the Thai and Malaysian communists, the Central Committee of Singapore's People's Party also quoted Mao by way of self-encouragement: "A weak nation can defeat a strong, a small nation can defeat a big ... if only they dare to rise in struggle, ... to take up arms."[155] Emulation of the Chinese model was emphatically reaffirmed in mid-1971 when the VMR pledged the "profound militant friendship" of the Malayan Communist Party with the Chinese Com-

munists. Paying tribute to *both Mao and Lin Piao,* the VMR assured
its audience in Malaysia and Singapore that the Chinese Communists'
experience in armed struggle was a historical model to be followed
and that Peking was the faithful ally of revolutionaries everywhere.[156]

Throughout 1970, frequently reports of guerrilla activities in
Sarawak and on the Malaysian-Thai border emanated from Kuala
Lumpur as well as from communist sources—the latter again including both Peking's official news agency and the Peking-sponsored
VMR.[157] As before, the official announcements spoke of "terrorist
sightings," discovery of guerrilla training centers, camps, and storage
areas, and redoubled government efforts to wipe out the insurgents.
The late Tun Ismail played an important role in a renewed Malaysian
effort to increase cooperation with Thailand, including the handling
of "hot pursuit" of guerrillas operating on the Malaysian-Thai border.
From the communist side there were the usual counterclaims of successful ambushes, success in eluding government forces, "mine warfare," and other exploits of the "Malayan National Liberation Army"
and the "North Kalimantan people's armed forces." These reports
continued during 1971.

(b) Nonmilitary attacks: As government forces began to gain on
the guerrillas during 1971, other anti-government themes became
more clearly defined and were expanded. Outside of the habitual call
for continued armed revolution, we can at least distinguish the following topics of long standing:

First, the Malaysian authorities were accused of fanning a Malay
chauvinism which wrecked national industrial and commercial enter-
prises. According to the VMR, whose alleged views in this case were
given wide circulation by NCNA, the "people's board of trust" was
one of the means designed to accelerate the growth of "Malay bureaucratic capital" at the expense of all other nationalities.[158] The VMR
and NCNA claimed that Malaysian authorities deliberately deprived
"Chinese, Indian, and other nationalities of their citizenship and their
right to work" on the ground that the latter's work permits had
expired.[159] "The Rahman–Razak clique" was held responsible for
"spreading national hatred ... by saying that Malaya belongs to the
Malays and not to the various nationalities, and that the Malay language is the only official language." All this was said to be a Malaysian

government attempt to prepare public opinion for a major racial outbreak and massacre.[160] While deliberately baiting both Malays and non-Malays in this manner, the VMR was quick to turn its wrath upon leaders of the Malayan Chinese Association who appealed for Chinese unity as a basis of national unity and loyalty to Malaysia.[161] Both Peking and the local communists had been consistently opposed to the emergence of a new Malaysian identity and were doing their best to exploit latent racial animosities.

A second traditional object of attack during this period was U. S. and British imperialism and "monopoly capital." Japan, however, was being increasingly linked to the same line of attack as the "vanguard of U. S. imperialism" in the latter's Asian "aggression." U. S. and Japanese capitalists were said to have infiltrated more and more into Malaya—meaning Malaysia as well as Singapore—with the cooperation of the governments of the two countries. The theme of exploitation of the poor by "bureaucratic capital" was linked in this manner to sentiments of economic nationalism. All this was, of course, a rather natural development from the Communists' Marxist ideology; the guiding hand of Peking's theory can also be detected. The shifting emphasis on Japan anticipated future attacks based on the alleged resurgence of Japanese militarism.

A third target was "Soviet revisionism," not only as a part of the broader Sino-Soviet conflict, but with special reference to Malaysia and Singapore. "Politically," said the VMR, "Soviet revisionist social-imperialism strongly supports the Rahman–Razak and Lee Kuan Yew cliques by tactically advising them and encouraging them in further suppression of the communists, opposing China, and opposing the people."[162] As a result of Tun Razak's visit to Moscow in 1968, speculated the VMR while referring to "Western Press" reports, "the Soviet revisionists ... promised to provide more than 100 million U. S. dollars worth of military equipment to the Rahman–Razak clique to oppress the armed struggle of the Malayan and the North Kalimantan peoples."[163] Razak was said to be willing to discuss arms aid with Russia.

Economically, the Soviet Union—which had a trade deficit with Malaysia—was accused of despoiling the country by buying tin, rubber, and other raw materials while its exports to the area were much smaller. The establishment of air services linking Kuala Lumpur and Singapore with Moscow, Soviet offers of low-interest loans, and the formation of a joint shipping company between the Soviet Union and Singapore were indicated as evidence of Soviet infiltration.[164]

Malaysia's Approach to Peking, 1970–71. Interestingly enough, it was against this background of armed and unarmed attacks on a broad front by the communists, openly encouraged by Peking's official mouthpiece, that Kuala Lumpur made its first open move toward Peking. The Malaysian initiative dated from October 1970, immediately after the formation of the Razak government. It was not preceded by a great deal of public discussion, as was the case in Thailand, nor was it followed by frequent reversals of position characteristic of the Thai–Peking dialogue. This new policy was by no means carried out without misgivings, however. The process slowly developed through the next two years. It straddled the period divisions which have been advanced in the introduction to this study, time spans readily applicable to Thailand: viz., the Nixon announcement of mid-1971, the entry of Peking into the United Nations, and the Shanghai communiqué.

Heralding the new Malaysian policy toward Communist China was the declaration of the new Prime Minister, Tun Abdul Razak—formerly Deputy to Tunku Rahman—that Malaysia would strive for non-alignment and non-involvement with any power bloc.[165] Since success of this policy requires Peking's non-interference with the sovereignty and internal affairs of Malaysia, the Razak government sought early contact with the Chinese Communists through Rumania.[166] There followed a declaration of support for the "immediate admission" of Peking to the United Nations. Malaysia was even prepared to cosponsor such a resolution; it was now opposed to the longstanding U. S. insistence on a two-thirds majority vote. "We want her [i.e., the PRC] to be admitted by a direct motion with a simple majority vote," said Tun Ismail, Deputy Prime Minister and head of the 1970 Malaysian delegation to the United Nations.[167] Dr. Ismail substantially tempered this seemingly pro-Peking position, however, by indicating that Malaysia would abstain on any move to expel Nationalist China from the United Nations. In his view, the PRC and Taiwan were two different nations. While Peking should be given the seat of China, the people on Taiwan should have the right of self-determination.[168] Further explanations by Prime Minister Razak suggested that his government was prepared to test the thesis, shared by optimists in many countries, that Peking would realize its international responsibilities once it became a member of the United Nations and subject to the influence of world opinion.[169]

Three months passed after Razak's initiative without any response from Peking. At the Singapore Commonwealth Prime Ministers' Conference in January 1971 Malaysia appealed for support from other Commonwealth members, including Canada and Zambia, asking them to explain to Peking the Malaysian proposal for neutralization of Southeast Asia[170] and, presumably, the Malaysian position on Chinese representation in the UN.

The first faint signal of a Chinese response arrived on February 10, 1971, in the form of a Chinese Red Cross offer of 625,000 Malaysian dollars to aid flood victims in Malaysia.[171] Although the offer was made in a telegram to the Malaysian Red Cross Society, it was regarded by government authorities as an indication of a change in Peking's policy toward the country itself.[172] At the same time, Malaysian Foreign Ministry officials noted publicly that since the beginning of 1971 Peking had spoken of *Malaysia* rather than *Malaya,* and that it had curtailed anti-Malaysian broadcasts.[173]

Perhaps the Red Cross signal was not strong enough. Perhaps there was internal opposition to one-sided concessions. One indication that Malaysia might be having second thoughts came when Tan Sri Ghazali Shafie, a government minister, told the Alliance Party that Malaysia was prepared to wait. It would respond positively to any indication of a *genuine desire* on the part of Peking to develop a mutually respectful relationship between the two countries.[174] A month later, in March 1971, even the Prime Minister was reported to have told an interviewer that while Malaysia maintained the same position on China, Peking was still helping the insurgents and "working against our established government with a view to subverting us."[175]

Addressing the House of Representatives on March 12, 1971, Razak restated Malaysia's China policy as follows: First, Malaysia recognized Peking as the legitimate government of China. However, the people of Taiwan should be given the right of self-determination. Second, it still remained for Peking to recognize Malaysia as an independent state and to conform to other international codes of conduct.[176] This was an indirect accusation that the PRC was still interfering with Malaysia's internal affairs by supporting the insurgents. The Malaysian policy could be further interpreted to mean that there would be no diplomatic recognition of Peking so long as the latter's support of Malaysian insurgents continued. In the absence of diplomatic recognition, Malaysia would also continue to maintain restrictions on travel to mainland China by its citizens with the exception of those seeking medical treatment.[177]

Malaysia did not wait too long, however, before resuming its test of Communist China's attitude. Following a government statement in early April 1971 that it was prepared to consider a privately-sponsored trade delegation to mainland China, an application was promptly received from the United Chamber of Commerce.[178] Permission was quickly granted and a nineteen-man mission led by Tengku Razaleigh and including four government officials left Hong Kong for China on May 8, 1971, less than a month after official announcement of the application. The mission's announced objective was to increase Malaysian exports to China because of the decline of Peking's rubber purchases from Malaysia in the preceding year.[179]

The first trade mission was successful. Upon his return to Kuala Lumpur on May 18, Tengku Razaleigh announced that Peking had agreed to increase its rubber purchases from Malaysia to 150,000–200,000 tons a year while Malaysia would import Chinese foodstuffs, light machinery, and farm equipment. The two parties also had agreed to trade directly rather than through some third party, and an invitation was extended to the Chinese Communists to send a similar trade mission on a return visit. Above all, however, Chou En-lai declared in a fifty-five minute interview with Tengku Razaleigh that he (Chou) "*welcomed in principle* [italics added] Malaysia's policy on the neutralization of Southeast Asia to be guaranteed by the big powers."[180] Furthermore, Chou was said to have referred to *Malaysia* instead of *Malaya* during the entire conversation, and to have sent his greetings to the King of Malaysia and to Tun Razak. The return visit of a Chinese trade mission in August was announced two months later by the chairman of the United Chamber of Commerce.[181]

Although Tun Razak was "encouraged" by the Chinese reception of the Malaysian trade mission and thought that Peking had begun to change its attitude toward Malaysia, certain reservations remained. First, the Secretary General of the Ministry of Foreign Affairs stated immediately after the mission's return that the government would not abandon its intention to wipe out domestic communist insurgency, in spite of increased contacts with Peking.[182] Second, Malaysia's position on diplomatic recognition remained unchanged. Peking must first recognize the independence and territorial integrity of Malaysia. The last point was reiterated by Tun Razak in Parliament on July 21. The long-standing communist insurgency and continuation of Peking's and VMR's anti-government statements proved to be more eloquent and persuasive than Chou En-lai's personal greetings and approval in principle of Malaysia's neutralization scheme.

The unofficial PRC trade delegation arrived in August, stayed for six days, and offered to buy "promptly" 40,000 tons of rubber, 5,000 tons of palm oil, and 50,000 cubic meters of logs.[183] In return, Malaysia promised to send technical experts to Communist China to provide advice on the use of standard Malaysian rubber.[184] A Malaysian trade delegation then went to the Canton trade fair, and an agreement was reached between the Chinese and Pernas—the Malaysian state trading organization—on methods of clearing and on settlement of trade balances.[185] By the end of 1971, however, these increased contacts had failed to bring the two sides together on the issue of diplomatic recognition.

In the meantime, the VMR, speaking in behalf of Peking, criticized the Malaysian government for its stand on Taiwan. Referring to a speech by the Malaysian Prime Minister on July 26, the VMR stated on August 28, 1971: "Razak claimed that his policy is not one of 'two Chinas' or 'one China, one Taiwan.' What he has said in this connection is actually more stupid than a marker posted by a thief saying that 'the missing treasure is not buried here.' "[186] The Malaysian response was more than a little confusing. As reported by the Kuala Lumpur radio on September 6, Tan Sri Zaiton of the Foreign Ministry maintained that Malaysia subscribed to a one China policy and not a two China or a one China–one Taiwan stand.[187] The Prime Minister, on the other hand, while acknowledging that Malaysia recognized only one China and would support the PRC's admission to the United Nations, less than two weeks later said that "Taiwan was a separate issue."[188]

At the United Nations Malaysia finally voted both against the U. S. resolution for dual representation and for the Albanian resolution to oust the Republic of China (ROC). True to its "one China," not "one China–one Taiwan" promise, Malaysia's position in October 1971 marked a significant change from the policy announced by Dr. Ismail a year earlier: that Malaysia would abstain from voting to oust Taiwan.

From 1972 to May 1974

Subsequent events showed that *either* the degree of change in Malaysian policy toward China was insufficient from Peking's point of view, *or* Peking was unwilling *and/or* unable to put a stop to its standing policy to support insurgency in *Malaya.* At any rate, the VMR, broadcasting in Malay to Singapore and Malaysia, again spoke of the "towering crimes of the Razak and Lee Kuan Yew cliques" perpetrated during 1971, including their "military offenses against the people in rural areas, in central Perak, northern Perak, southern Kedah, and northern Kelantan." It commended the determination of the Malayan National Liberation Army "to wipe out the enemy's effectives, expand the army and militia organization, [and] constantly develop the base and guerrilla areas."[189] It also described the Razak government as having "flirted with the U. S. running dogs in other Asian countries." To quote a later broadcast, "the Thanom–Praphat traitorous clique, the Suharto fascist regime, and the Pak Chong-hui clique are all closely colluding with the Razak clique to serve the U. S. imperialists' war policies."[190] If there was any faint indication of a change in attitude, one could point to the following sentence in the same broadcast: "The criminal activities of the Razak clique in supporting the Lon Nol–Sirik Matak clique politically . . . are regarded by them as in line with *Malaysia's* [italics added] independent foreign policy."[191] At least the VMR used the term "Malaysia"!

Three months later, this time speaking out specifically against Singapore, the VMR accused Prime Minister Lee Kuan Yew of being "active in selling out state sovereignty and national interests."[192] It pointed to Singapore's economic policy of inviting foreign investments and its general use of the English language in education. If the Nixon–Chou communiqué indicated Peking's agreement against the attainment of regional hegemony by any power in Asia, the understanding obviously did not extend to "indigenous revolutionary movements" whose objective, if attained, would result in the establishment of a *Malayan*—or *Malaysian*—regime sympathetic to Peking.

A new constitution of the Communist Party of Malaya was made public toward the end of May.[193] It spoke of "Marxist–Leninist–Mao Tse-tung thought as the guide for its ideology," and of its own experiences as proof that "the path of encircling cities from the countryside and seizing political power by armed force" was "the only correct line." Although reports of insurgent activities had become less frequent, they were by no means totally absent. In East Malaysia there were some joint counterinsurgency operations by Malaysia and Indonesia.[194] By the end of the year, however, Dr. Ismail, the Deputy Prime Minister, was reported to have stated in parliament that the communists were "no longer a threat to the state" and that they were contained in Sarawak.[195]

In the midst of continuing VMR attacks and apparently reduced guerrilla activities—probably a result of reduced capability—Peking's NCNA continued its reports on revolutionary successes in various Asian countries and, albeit less frequently, on successful exploits of insurgents in Malaysia.[196] Nor did it entirely abandon its use of the term *Malaya* in referring to Malaysia and Singapore. Peking also reported the visits to Peking of Malaysian doctors and delegates from the Malaysian Table Tennis Association, each time referring to *Malaysia*.[197] Whenever Peking's anti-Soviet interest was served, Communist China was prepared even to cite the Malaysian government's stand short of open endorsement. This occurred when a Soviet proposal to internationalize the Straits of Malacca met with Malaysian opposition. "Malaysian Prime Minister Tun Abdul Razak . . . stressed that it was up to Malaysia and Indonesia," reported NCNA, "to decide whether or not the narrow waterway should be internationalized."[198]

On the Malaysian side, in addition to the visits of special groups to Peking, Malaysian diplomats were given official permission to attend the PRC's National Day celebrations in Vienna.[199] A trade mission led by Tun Sri Raja Mohar was sent to Peking in November and was reported at the time to be entrusted with non-economic goals—including discussion of the ultimate "normalization of relations" between the two countries.[200] Obviously, Malaysia could not be immune from the examples set earlier in the year by Japan, Australia, and New Zealand in the train of events set in motion by

President Nixon's new China policy and its mode of implementation.

However, contrary to what many observers might have expected, Malaysia in reality was far slower in its approach to Peking and far more cautious than, for instance, Japan. Diplomatic relations had not been established between Malaysia and the PRC by the end of 1973 although the imminence of "normalization" was periodically reported during the year. Indicative of changed power relationships in this part of the world was a Moscow Radio commentary on January 5, 1974, describing as naïve and unrealistic the hope any country might have that recognition could persuade Peking to cease its support of insurgency. In this connection, reference was made by the Soviet commentator to the experience of both India and Burma, whose diplomatic relations with Peking proved to be no obstacle to PRC support of insurgents—and worse—in both countries.

Rapprochement with Peking in May 1974

The final plunge by Malaysia was made in May 1974 when Tun Razak visited Peking. A Chou En-lai–Razak joint communiqué issued on May 31 established full diplomatic relations between Peking and Kuala Lumpur. According to *The New York Times* (June 1, 1974), Peking stated in the communiqué that it regarded all Malaysian citizens of Chinese origin to be Malaysians and urged all Chinese citizens in Malaysia to obey Malaysian laws. Peking, however, made no mention of Chinese support for the Malayan Communist Party and the VMR, although the *People's Daily* had stated on May 24—doubtless for Razak's benefit—that all nations should handle their own affairs. Peking's profession of a hands-off attitude toward Kuala Lumpur's Malaynization policy at long last may have been prompted by its increased anxiety to "leap frog" Thailand, which had been unusually tenacious in its resistance to Chinese overtures. India's nuclear detonation and the rise of Soviet power in the Indian Ocean may have strengthened the Chinese desire to establish a foothold on the land ridge dividing the Indian and Pacific Oceans as soon as possible.

For Malaysia, the degree of concession offered by Peking was apparently sufficient. However, only a few days after Razak's return the Malaysian police chief was assassinated by terrorists in what appeared to be a signal of the continuation of insurgent activities in spite of the Chou–Razak communiqué.

Malaysia and Singapore: the Communal Problem and Relations with Peking

One conclusion emerging clearly from the preceding account of the evolution of Malaysian-Peking relations is the PRC's pursuit of its external relations at two different levels: The official level attempts to exploit such relations or their apparent improvement or deterioration for strategic, political, and economic benefit under changing international conditions. The ideological and party level consistently preaches armed struggle, the inevitable success of revolution, fraternal relations with revolutionary movements everywhere, the strategy of "surrounding cities by the countryside" interpreted broadly, and the need to build an internal base of support for revolution or the principle of "self-reliance."

The clear implementation of both approaches, however, is subject to certain constraints. First, at any given time the Chinese decision-makers themselves may not be in agreement, and unequivocal decisions cannot be made outright. Second, the exact locus of the authority to make new decisions may not be undisputed. Third, in the absence of clear and energetic guidance from undisputed authority, inertia and resistance to change are likely to take over. Fourth, because of its weaker position in terms of real military and economic power in relation to both the Soviet Union and the United States, Peking cannot abandon its revolutionary stance without giving up its claim to leadership in parts of the third world and in the international revolutionary movements. Its external posture at the ideological and party level requires militancy as working capital. A revisionist Peking would be a poor second in any contest with the Soviet Union. Fifth, given the existence of local insurgents and their will to continue the struggle, Peking may not be able to stop them even if it were willing to try. Finally, Mao Tse-tung and his associates are genuine revolutionaries and probably have no intention to try to curb what they believe to be the inexorable march of history.

The Malaysian position is no less complex. From the Malaysian point of view—and, as pointed out earlier, also the Thai point of view—normal state relations with Peking, including mutual diplomatic relations, would be beneficial if such relations were regarded by local communists as Peking's endorsement of the existing government. This would be reinforced if Peking would urge its local followers to change their attitude toward the government. Peking could take advantage of such state relations, however, to further its external policy at the ideological and party level to the detriment of the government. The presence of a PRC diplomatic mission in the country could make this problem even more serious. Once diplomatic relations were established, moreover, their suspension would be a most serious step in reverse, far worse in exacerbating relations with Peking than postponement of full recognition.

Since 1969, the state of insurgency and the degree of success of counterinsurgency measures affected the Malaysian government in different ways. On the one hand, the less intense the insurgency, the less the government's need to use relations with Peking as an aid to counterinsurgency. On the other hand, with an increase in internal stability, the government would have less to fear from PRC interference and diplomatic presence. Since these considerations pull in opposite directions, subjective assessment by policy-makers becomes very important. The nature of the leadership's perception cannot be divorced from the leaders as individuals. The succession of Tun Razak to Tunku Rahman thus had a significant effect.

If there is less need to enlist Peking's aid *vis-à-vis* the insurgents, why should closer relations with Peking be sought at all, even if such a relationship would also be potentially less dangerous? The answer seems to lie in Razak's idea about the neutralization of Southeast Asia as a means of gaining big-power guarantees. The desire for neutralization as a means of safeguarding security stems from Malaysia's perception of the effect, first, of the British withdrawal from east of the Suez and, second, of the U. S. disengagement from Vietnam and the Washington–Peking rapprochement. If no Western power strong enough to afford protection to Malaysia is going to be on the scene, the latter must reduce Peking's potential hostility. But how far and how quickly Malaysia dares to go in this direction cannot be easily determined because of the uncertainty inherent in assessing the net effect of closer relations with Peking. The problem is complicated both by the PRC's pursuit of external relations at two different levels and by the one fundamental internal problem confronting Malaysia.

This fundamental issue is the fact that Malaysia has not yet achieved full success in integrating its ethnic Chinese minority into the nation. The expulsion of Singapore from the Federation, the May 1969 riot, and the preference given to Malays in employment and education—which was intended to create a better racial balance— have hindered the development of racial harmony and a uniform national consciousness and identity. Malaysian recognition of this state of affairs may have contributed to the continuation of a semi- official relationship between Malaysia and Taiwan up to June 1974.[201] So long as some of the Chinese elements in Malaysia are sympathetic to Taiwan, it would benefit the Malaysian authorities to maintain a balancing Chinese influence to counter that of Peking. If Taiwan were to become an independent nation, it would be even more beneficial to Malaysia since the potential attraction of Peking would be diluted and an example would be set for the development of a new national identity by ethnic Chinese outside the orbit of mainland China.

The role of Malay-Chinese relations in Malaysia also affects signi- ficantly the security of Singapore and, indirectly, PRC–Singapore rapport. Already noted is the hostility of Peking and the Malayan Communist Party toward the Singapore government. Because of its small size and its effective maintenance of internal security, however, Singapore has no active insurgents. So long as it can keep Peking at arm's length it is not faced with a direct Chinese threat, although its multi-racial population (predominantly Chinese) has the urgent need of developing a Singaporean identity. This is perhaps a somewhat less intractable task than that facing Malaysia. However, should communal riots again develop in Malaysia, racial affinity may create an overwhelming popular demand for intervention. In this hypo- thetical situation, if the ethnic Chinese in Malaysia should become identified with resurgent communist "terrorists" in their own minds and/or in the eyes of Malaysian authorities, Singapore may become more involved with Peking than it desires. As long as racial peace is maintained on the Malay Peninsula, and as long as Singapore is successful in creating a new national identity, relations with the PRC are viewed by Singapore primarily in the context of balance of power.

— 3 —

PRC Relations with Indonesia

Before the Cultural Revolution

In contrast to its relations with the other countries discussed in this paper, on the eve of the Cultural Revolution Peking not only enjoyed a close relationship with Indonesia, but was rapidly shaping its liaison with Sukarno into a semi-alliance. When the latter withdrew the Indonesian delegation from the United Nations on January 2, 1965, Peking's official publication praised his "revolutionary, bold action" and castigated the U. S. and British "imperialists" for their effort to use Malaysia as a "bridgehead" to "overawe and attack Indonesia."[202] An orchestrated, nationwide campaign to support Indonesia and condemn the United Nations took place in China through newspapers and mass organizations. NCNA quoted the chairman of the Indonesian Communist Party, D. N. Aidit, as giving his unreserved support to Sukarno on January 9.[203] Two days later the PRC Foreign Minister and Vice Premier, Chen I, spoke of Indonesia's "just, revolutionary move."[204] Chen praised Sukarno's leadership in promoting the Asian-African cause of anti-imperialism and anti-colonialism, and linked the latest Sukarno gesture to the convergence of "the revolutionary movements of the people of the world" into "an irresistible historical torrent."[205] All this rhetoric was more than a routine endorsement of Indonesia.

Peking's real intentions were revealed by Chou En-lai in a speech later in the month when he explained Communist China's attitude toward Malaysia as well as his hopes for the developing PRC-Indonesian relationship. "'Malaysia,'" said Chou, "is an artificial creation of Britain in collusion with the United States. It is well known that there exists a Malaya on this globe, but not such a thing as 'Malaysia.' The so-called 'Malaysia' is something which Britain imposes on the people of Malaya, Singapore, Sarawak and Sabah in order to perpetuate its colonial rule.... In making 'Malaysia' to include Sarawak and Sabah, Britain is in effect planting a bayonet in the chest of the Republic of Indonesia."[206]

After justifying Indonesia's opposition to Malaysia in this manner, Chou then argued that the seating of Malaysia in the United Nations and the Security Council was more evidence of the misuse of the United Nations by the United States and Britain. Hence, the United Nations should be reorganized as Sukarno had long proposed. However, reorganization of the United Nations had not been possible up to that time because countries like Communist China, North Korea, and North Vietnam were not in the organization, while many members either had U. S. military bases on their soil or were not really independent nations. "In these circumstances," concluded Chou, "another United Nations, a revolutionary one, may well be set up so that rival dramas may be staged in competition with that body which calls itself the United Nations."[207]

In the name of a PRC-Indonesian partnership, Peking's foreign policy plans as of 1965 would seem to include the use of Indonesia as an instrument in furthering Communist China's goal of leading an Asian-African or—on a broader scale—a "third world" group of countries in competition with the two super-powers. Such an arrangement, if realized, would have become the culmination of a foreign policy approach initiated by Chou En-lai at Bandung ten years earlier. Within a regional context, however, it would have given Peking the added advantage of having an ally at the other end of the South China Sea. A Peking–Jakarta axis would have placed three of the land ridge countries—Thailand, Malaysia, and Singapore—in the middle. In Peking's eyes, Indochina was already well on its way toward being "liberated."

The PRC apparently intended to do considerably more than offer Indonesia moral support in their joint undertaking. According to Liu Shao-ch'i, then chief of state and still Mao's heir apparent, "The Chinese people would consider it an honor... if they could make some contributions to Indonesia's self-reliance," which was regarded as the correct policy for newly independent nations.[208] Further discussion of what the PRC could do to help presumably took place in late January between Subandrio, Chou En-lai, and Chen I. Indicative of the nature of these discussions was the list of Chinese participants. Included were the chief of staff of the People's Liberation Army (PLA), his deputy, the commander of the Chinese navy, the deputy commander of the air force, and a vice minister of public security (intelligence and secret police), in addition to the usual foreign affairs and trade officials.[209] "The Chinese people," Peking's then chief of staff, Lo Jui-ch'ing, was reported as saying, "firmly supported [the] Indonesian people's struggle to confront 'Malaysia.'"[210] Echoing the same sentiment at "a happy get-together," as the meeting was described by the Indonesian navy commander, Vice Admiral Maya Martadinata replied: "The armed forces of Indonesia and China have a common revolutionary task: to firmly oppose imperialism and old and new colonialism."[211]

Between January and the end of September 1965, when the Indonesian Communist Party (PKI) staged its abortive coup against the predominantly anti-communist elements in the military, Peking's relationship with the Sukarno government was being progressively tightened. Members of the Indonesian Defense Institute visited Peking on September 28–29 and held talks with the PRC National Defense Council.[212] Several other Indonesian groups were also in China at that time. On September 30, the day the coup took place, a Sino-Indonesian agreement for economic and technical cooperation was signed, together with specific protocols on trade and payment.[213] Two days after the coup Subamia, Vice Speaker of the Indonesian Cooperation Parliament, said in Peking that "no imperialist sabotage could disrupt the unity between China and Indonesia."[214] His reference to "imperialist sabotage" hinted at the line the PKI and its sympathizers planned to take in explaining the coup had it been successful.

There was a breakdown of communications between Peking and its friends and agents in Indonesia. According to NCNA, the agency lost contact with its correspondents in Indonesia between October 1 and 16.[215] Until the middle of that month Peking probably thought the coup had been successful. Lack of information and mistaken judgment were apparently at the root of some otherwise inexplicable statements made by Peking during the first half of October. For some time after that, Peking may have thought it still possible to salvage its relationship with Indonesia through Sukarno.

During the first week of October various groups of Indonesian visitors—including members of the Defense Institute, the Air Academy, and educational and trade organizations—hurriedly returned home. As late as October 7, however, PRC authorities still saw fit to release a joint statement of the Standing Committee of the National People's Congress and the Indonesian People's Assembly although the delegation from Indonesia had left three days earlier. "Both parties," stated the communiqué, "reaffirm their support for the national liberation movements of the peoples of Asia, Africa, and Latin America, and for the new emerging forces in their struggle to smash the domination of the United States-led imperialists and to build a new society free from exploitation and oppression. . . . Both parties pledge their continued support for the people of Malaya and North Kalimantan in fighting for national liberation, and hold that the struggle against 'Malaysia' must be kept up till complete victory."[216]

According to NCNA's report, on October 18, 1965, elements of the Indonesian armed forces had entered the Chinese Commercial Counsellor's office in Jakarta. This was followed by similar incidents involving the living quarters of PRC embassy staff, Chinese textile experts in Indonesia, the NCNA office, the PRC consulate at Medan, etc. Altogether, there were at least nine official protests from the PRC Embassy to the Indonesian Foreign Ministry during the last two months of the year."[217] Peking continued to hope for the return of Sukarno to power and that of the PKI to a position of influence, however, as may be witnessed in the presence of PRC representatives at the International Conference on Liquidation of Foreign Military Bases which took place in Jakarta on October 17–20. Even later, Peking apparently still held the idea that Sukarno might win out. Only when power shifted to Suharto in March 1966 and the NCNA office in Jakarta was closed did Peking let loose its propaganda directly against the Indonesian government. Peking's plans for Indonesia had effectively collapsed at the end of 1965, however, and a total reversal of the relationship between the two countries was about to begin.

After the Cultural Revolution

Failure of the PKI-sponsored coup did not lead to the immediate assumption of power by the anti-communists or to the total eclipse of Sukarno. Only in March 1966 was the latter forced to give General Suharto, whose forces crushed the revolt, full power to take whatever measures were necessary to restore law and order. Suharto immediately outlawed the PKI, formed a new cabinet, and assumed the portfolios of defense and security in addition to one of the seats of the three-man presidium. Dr. Adam Malik, a founding member of the National Marxist Party previously banned by Sukarno, took over foreign affairs. It was not until January 1967, however, that Anwar Sanusi—the last member of the Politburo of the PKI at large in Indonesia after the attempted coup—was finally arrested. Relations between Peking and Indonesia had further deteriorated in the interim. The PRC chargé d'affaires was expelled on April 24, 1967. Diplomatic relations between the two countries were suspended six months later. By 1969, when Peking began to reexamine its external policy, this state of suspended relationship had remained largely unchanged.

Indonesia's perception of Peking's intentions and mode of operation thus was strongly affected by the role Peking was believed to have played—and probably did play—during and after the coup. The following factors contributed to the Indonesian image of Peking:

First, the PRC was believed to have supplied arms to Indonesian communists. Indonesian newspapers reported in October 1965 that crates of weapons had been discovered among the equipment supplied by Communist China for the Conference of New Emerging Forces (CONEFO) which Sukarno planned to call in 1966.[218] The *Indonesian Herald* openly hinted on October 20, 1965, that Peking had conspired to impose its ideology on other nations. Vice Admiral Martadinata, who had been a recent visitor to Peking, thought that the coup definitely received foreign aid.[219]

Second, according to Njono—a member of the PKI Politburo and former chairman of the PKI-controlled trade union organization—D. N. Aidit had spoken of communist plans to seize power at the end of August 1965.[220] Earlier in the year, in the name of defense against Malaysia, Aidit had called for arming the "workers and peasants."

Aidit was a frequent visitor to Peking which, through NCNA on December 2, 1965, praised the Indonesian as the "outstanding helmsman" in the PKI.

Third, the only PKI Politburo member at large in 1967, Jusuf Adjitorop, was being built up by Peking as a spokesman of the Indonesian PKI at a time when Peking's relations with Indonesia were reaching the breaking point.

Fourth, more than once in the past Peking had protested vigorously against Indonesia's maltreatment of "overseas Chinese." Because of the connection of Peking and the Indonesian Chinese to the 1965 coup, similar protests after the coup had the side-effect of exacerbating communal relations.[221] Even if unintended, the cynic might argue that this could have the effect of discrediting the Suharto leadership, thus making the country's economic plight worse. National unrest might return the PKI to power.

From the Indonesian point of view, then, the PRC was an active supporter of a communist coup which nearly succeeded. Furthermore, Peking was obviously supporting an anti-Indonesian government communist group in exile. Lastly, Peking was not above exploiting the ethnic Chinese in Indonesia; its political and ideological interest was potentially in conflict with improvement of racial relations, a necessary condition for economic stability and development.

1969. Given such a view of Communist China, the fact that diplomatic relations between the two countries had been suspended for some time, and the collapse of the domestic communists, there was no good reason for the Indonesian government to be anxious for a rapprochement with Peking. If Indonesian security was affected by U. S. troop withdrawals from Asia, there were other options to be pursued than an approach to the Chinese communists.

In response to President Nixon's Guam speech, Foreign Minister Adam Malik noted in August 1969 that Indonesia had never been dependent upon the United States or Britain and would, therefore, suffer no direct impact from U. S. troop withdrawals from Southeast Asia or the British withdrawal from east of the Suez.[222] What Indonesia needed was a stronger economy and national ideology, as well as greater ability to defend itself. National resilience in all Southeast Asian countries should be consolidated through regional and subregional organizations. As for the communist nations from which Indonesia had become estranged, according to Malik, the Soviet Union was now ready to resume construction of development projects in Indonesia which had been suspended after the fall of Sukarno and to postpone debt repayment by Indonesia.

A different case was presented by the PRC. The Indonesian news agency quoted Malik as saying, "While things are progressing well in China, sometime in the future the Chinese government will be more aware of her bigger responsibility towards the world...and subsequently will pursue a foreign policy that is less aggressive and more mature."[223] If China wanted to prosper, her government would have to adapt its policy to developments in neighboring countries. Resumption of aid to PKI remnants would not be in the PRC's national interest. Malik thought that a distinction should be made between the Chinese Communist Party and the PRC government, however, suggesting that while the communist party might be ideologically unacceptable, the communist government of a nation–state could conceivably become less aggressive and therefore acceptable.

Indonesia's position on Taiwan, as outlined by Malik in 1969, resembled that of Malaysia. "If we recognize Nationalist China, it would be justifying Chinese colonial hold on Taiwan." This obviously meant that there should be "one China and one Taiwan."[224]

Before and After the U. S. July 1971 Announcement. There was very little change in Jakarta–Peking relations during 1970. Indonesian sensitivity to PRC interference in the country's internal affairs was demonstrated in a report on the presence of Chinese visitors on Buru Island, where political prisoners of Category B working on an agricultural project were held in detention camps.[225] The report mentioned three former PKI members as the ringleaders of twenty-five hundred prisoners who attempted to sabotage the project and to make "a Marxist training camp" on Buru. "In addition," the report continued, "there are non-Indonesian Chinese, disguised as merchants, who are coming to Buru, ostensibly to buy the farms' produce grown at the camps. *All land, sea, and air access routes therefore must be closely watched, for security's sake, to prevent the entry of such Chinese* [italics added]."[226]

The same attitude continued to prevail in the spring of 1971 in

spite of new signs of a U. S.–PRC rapprochement. Speaking to newsmen at Medan on April 15, 1971, Dr. Malik noted that "attempts
to normalize relations between Indonesia and China were never
stopped," but that "he saw no reason to accelerate the improvement
of the frozen ties."[227] The two standing conditions for normalization
were "that China cease subversive attempts in Indonesia and recognize the present Suharto administration as the legal Indonesian
Government."[228]

Reluctance to take any step toward resumption of diplomatic
relations, however, was not accompanied by reluctance to trade; nor
would the Indonesian government prohibit travel to Peking by an
Indonesian badminton team.[229] According to the Indonesian Foreign
Minister, Indonesian businessmen should be encouraged to trade
directly with Peking in exporting rubber, copra, peanut oil, etc.
Indonesia was clearly concerned about reported plans to reduce the
U. S. rubber stockpile and about the competition of Malaysian rubber
in view of PRC rubber purchases from Malaysia.[230]

Nevertheless, Indonesia's readiness to use sports as a gesture of
flexibility in external relations—emulating the United States—was not
accompanied by the kind of agonizing public reassessment Thailand
displayed after the Nixon announcement of mid-1971. The Indonesian Army, which had borne the brunt of the PKI blood bath in
1965, was not about to let down its guard. A statement to *Merdeka* by
General Maraden Panggabean, Deputy Commander of the Indonesia
Republican Armed Forces, was unmistakably clear on this point:
"We are not going to repeat the old order's political system with its
Jakarta–Pyongyang–Peking axis, which cost so many lives, nor are
we going to make any exceptions in establishing relations with
foreign countries."[231] Normalization of relations with any country
would not be possible so long as that country continued to adopt an
attitude damaging to Indonesia's national security. There could be
no exception to this rule.

As expressed by Dr. Malik a month and a half before the actual
vote in New York, Indonesia's attitude toward the issue of Chinese
representation before the United Nations was equally uncompromis-
ing. Dr. Malik reportedly stated at a meeting with Prime Minister
Sato in Tokyo that Indonesia shared the Japanese position in principle; namely, it hoped to see both Peking and Taiwan seated in the

United Nations.[232] When the votes were finally counted on October 26, 1971, Indonesia voted with the United States, Japan, and Thailand, among others, in favor of the "important matter" resolution.[233] When this resolution was defeated by fifty-nine to fifty-four, Indonesia abstained from the Albanian resolution to expel Taiwan and seat Peking, as did Thailand. They did not vote with the United States and Japan against the Albanian resolution.

Through 1970 and 1971 Peking's position was equally unbending. To the PRC and its official press, the post-Sukarno government was a "fascist military clique" serving U. S. interests in Southeast Asia that "begged" for foreign aid to support its economy.[234] This was the same attitude Peking had shown Thailand.

The Shanghai Communiqué and Thereafter

On the eve of Mr. Nixon's visit to Peking, President Suharto told the press in Canberra that normalization of relations between Indonesia and Peking still depended upon the latter's willingness to "stop its slanders" against Indonesia.[235] General Suharto also told the assembled newsmen that there was enough evidence of Peking's active involvement in the "PKI 30 September incident." Against this background, Indonesia's official response to the Shanghai communiqué was that national resilience had to be strengthened.[236] There was, however, no immediate concern paralleling that of Thailand.[237] It was not until August 1972, when the Thai National Executive Council decided to send a badminton team to Peking in response to the latter's invitation, that Malik publicly spoke of the Thai government's decision as "a promising step toward the opening of talks between the two countries."[238] As was the case in Thailand, the Indonesian government was probably divided in its evaluation of the prospects. Other advisors close to General Suharto were reportedly prepared to watch even longer for new developments than was Dr. Malik.

Indonesia was plainly cautious and mindful of its past experience. It was not willing to take initiative in a direction that, in its view, could again lead to disaster. It resisted the idea that some third country might usefully serve as a go-between. In Malik's words,

Indonesia had no need for an intermediary to negotiate "normalization." The important thing was for Peking to realize that there was a new government in power in Indonesia, and that Peking should not assist the PKI remnants living in mainland China *or* aid subversives through overseas Chinese.[239]

According to Vice Admiral Subono, Chief of the General Staff of the Defense and Security Department, there was an increase in foreign-inspired subversion during 1972 and the threat from PKI remnants could not be ignored completely.[240] The Indonesian military's suspicion was intensified by the belief that an espionage network in Indonesia was supported by Communist China. This was stressed by General Sumrahadi, head of the Defense Security Information Center.[241] The espionage ring reportedly began operation in 1965 and was expanded in 1972.

There is some uncertainty about the exact role Japan either played or—perhaps more likely—*tried* to play as a mediator. A Japanese newspaper reported in September 1972 that the Indonesian government had unofficially requested Japan to act as an intermediary with a view to normalizing relations between Jakarta and Peking.[242] Dr. Malik indirectly refuted the report, however, in a comment on the Chou–Tanaka talks which had just taken place.[243] While expressing his hope that the Sino-Japanese agreement would lead to lessening of tension in Asia, Malik again noted that normalization of relations between Jakarta and Peking depended upon Peking, that Indonesia required no third-party intermediary, and that the Peking–Tokyo agreement should not influence other countries.[244] One hypothesis of these contradictions would be that Tanaka had actively sought to act as intermediary for Indonesia, or at least to have had the appearance of being one. It would have added to his own bargaining chips in dealing with Peking and avoided creating difficulties for Japan as a result of his new China policy, since Japan also needed to maintain good relations with Indonesia.

Malik's disavowal of any need for an intermediary was made clear in an interview, when he said that the PRC ambassador to the United Nations took part in an Indonesian independence day observance in New York in August 1972.[245] Several meetings were held between the two sides. On October 11, 1972, the Foreign Minister disclosed his impression that Communist China seemed to welcome normalization of relations with Indonesia. In his view Peking's statement on non-interference in the domestic affairs of other countries, which was highlighted in the Chou–Tanaka talks, would also be applicable to Indonesia.[246] Thus, in view of the timing, Indonesia was not uninfluenced by the Peking–Tokyo rapprochement. As of October 1972, however, Malik's position and that of others in authority was that Indonesia would not take any initiative; it would wait for Peking to make its position clear. Peking had yet to make itself credible as a peaceful neighbor.

Indonesian doubts about Peking's vague promise of good behavior were not easily allayed. Even after the preliminary contacts in New York, Indonesian immigration authorities continued to bar the reentry—either as visitors or as tourists—of PRC citizens who had been repatriated from Indonesia.[247] As the year 1972 ended, Malik still held that Indonesia was not yet ready to restore diplomatic relations with Peking. Such a step would have to be preceded by adequate domestic preparations safeguarding against any recurrence of "Chinese subversive activities."[248] Chou En-lai's reassurances were insufficient to convince Indonesia. Nor was Indonesia going to be swayed by a then-prevailing rumor about Malaysia's possible recognition of the PRC.[249]

Since anti-Chinese racial riots broke out in Bandung in the summer of 1973 and again in early 1974 during Tanaka's visit to Jakarta, it would appear that "internal preparations" were far from being complete. Barring a radical change in external conditions, more time must pass before a Peking–Jakarta rapprochement.

— 4 —

Counterbalance Versus Neutralization
in a Vacuum

In their approaches to foreign policy, a major difference between Malaysia and the other three countries we have examined is that while the former still harbors the hope of ensuring security by neutralization with major power guarantees, the latter seem to feel that no such major power agreement and self-restraint can be obtained before a coincidence of national interests has been developed. In the second approach, each of a sufficient number of major powers must first find itself unable to alter the status quo without incurring disproportionate cost. Second, each must also be strongly opposed to allowing others to alter the status quo. Third, each must find it not only inadvisable, but also unnecessary to make such an alteration itself. The third condition can be fulfilled only if the major power in question can derive some benefit from the status quo. The second condition can be satisfied when this benefit is substantial and must be safeguarded from the point of view of each major power lest it be excluded from the benefit if another major power became the predominant influence. The first condition can be satisfied if enough major powers can be balanced against one another through their simultaneous presence.

Our analysis in the preceding sections has shown that multilateral presence has gradually emerged in all four countries. Even in the case of Malaysia, while the goal of "instant neutralization" with major power guarantees may continue to be hailed as desirable, inability to attain this objective has not precluded the voluntary development of major-power presence by invitation.

71

There is a visible difference, however, in the degree to which the increasing presence of individual major powers is welcomed. In all instances there has been a remarkable aversion to greater PRC presence. The aversion is greatest in Singapore and Indonesia, but it is no less tangible in Thailand. Malaysia took its time before plunging headlong into diplomatic recognition of Peking. (Both Malaysia and Peking, however, had appeared to be on the brink of doing so more than once since 1971.) The Soviet Union is equally suspect, at least to Indonesia and Thailand. Here again Malaysia seems to be the exception, while Singapore is much more cautious. Finally, Japan is regarded as a potential major power, but—as personal discussions have shown repeatedly—there are (a) serious doubts about Japan's capability as a counterbalancing force, (b) real concern about potential Japanese militarism, and (c) more than a little uneasiness about the sharp practices of some Japanese businessmen.

Malaysia's dream of neutralization would probably be an ideal solution to the three other states if only it could be realized and well-founded. Past experience, however, suggests to their leaders that it is unrealistic to accept at face value Soviet and PRC assurances. In all instances they fear subversion through increasing Soviet and Chinese presence. Both Indonesia and Thailand have openly expressed their concern about any large Soviet presence. The general aversion to greater PRC presence is partly derived from Peking's doctrine and partly from its record of support for insurgency against the established governments in these countries. There are, of course, those who argue that better relations with Peking at the state level might soften the latter's attitude toward established authorities.[250] Even if this turns out to be true in particular instances, however, it may not be true in specific cases and it certainly cannot vouchsafe Peking's future policy. Only if one could count on the *stability* of benevolent behavior would this argument gain real persuasiveness in the eyes of the countries in question. It is they who must run the risk and bear the immediate consequences of erroneous judgment.

Concern about the PRC is augmented by the presence of large ethnic Chinese communities which—rightly or wrongly—make some of the government leaders fear that the PRC could infiltrate and subvert their countries more easily than the Russians. In the case of Singapore and Malaysia, which are both new countries, the relatively large proportion of ethnic Chinese in the entire population could add to the difficulty of creating lasting new national identities and loyalties. These effects of the existence of the Chinese racial elements obviously are beyond the power of Peking alone to correct. Even if the PRC had had an impeccable record of honoring its assurances, it would not be possible for these promises to appear credible so long as internal stability and/or national identity has not been fully established in these countries.

For this reason, too, the record shows that all four countries would really prefer to have the influence and attraction of the PRC contested and diluted by counter-attractions. Whatever their open protestations, therefore, the existence of Taiwan as a separate political entity would be in their national interest, and there is ample evidence that they knew that. They have not been able to give vent to their real preference for three primary reasons: (a) the continued claim of the Republic of China to the Chinese mainland; (b) for this reason, fear of incurring the open hostility of the PRC; and (c) uncertainty about the real U.S. policy toward China—i.e., whether Washington has in fact decided on giving up its support of Taiwan in order to court Peking. (This implies that Washington is not taken at its word.)

The very slow evolution of their relations with Peking on the part of all four countries since 1969 has clearly shown their universal reluctance to do so. Yet, with the exception of Indonesia, three have either developed or expanded direct trade relations and other contacts and—for Malaysia—even diplomatic recognition. In the case of Thailand, the shift to a less preferred position has been brought about by changes in the policy of the United States in Asia, i.e., Washington's rapprochement with Peking, the disengagement of U.S. ground forces from Vietnam, and U.S. passivity in regard to cease-fire violations by North Vietnam. In the case of Malaysia and Singapore, the same U.S. moves have aggravated a security problem initiated by the early announcement of British withdrawal from east of the Suez. In sort, the PRC is not really welcome. It may be necessary, however, to placate Peking because of these British and U.S. withdrawals.

Policy adjustments on the part of the four countries have been initiated during the 1969–74 period primarily in response to changes in U.S. and—secondarily—in the case of Malaysia and Singapore,

British policies. Looking ahead, however, a new set of responses may be in the offing. The likely responses to an increase in Soviet activities must now be considered. As the U. S.-British presence receded, the Soviet Union increased its cultural, trade, and other economic contacts. It has developed air links through civil aviation agreements and the extension of Aeroflot routes. It has established joint shipping services with Singapore and Malaysia. It has occasionally entered into direct trade competition with the PRC and even Japan.[251] During the 1971 Commonwealth Prime Ministers' Conference in Singapore, it enacted a scene described by some as "gunboat diplomacy." With the continued expansion of the Soviet navy and the reopening of the Suez Canal in the not too distant future, the Soviet Union will be in a more favorable position to pursue its exploitation of both the Indian and Pacific oceans and their littoral states within the context of its own global policy.

Thus far the Soviet Union has been singularly unsuccessful in developing its concept of Asian collective security. But it has not neglected preliminary preparations in terms of trade and air and sea communications as well as other contacts. Might its future endeavors be attended by greater success? Or does the Soviet Union really have no such ambitions or—even if it does—would it exercise self-restraint? To policy-makers in the four countries, greater Soviet presence and greater risk to themselves obviously must be expected.

If the PRC is an unwelcome countervailing force—rendered even less dependable and more capricious by its internal instability—and if Japan has become an even less promising prospect in this respect than before due to its uninspiring diplomatic performance during the 1973–74 energy crisis, what counterbalancing forces actually are available? Nationalism in the individual countries, aided by continued U. S. military presence in Southeast Asia, successfully slowed down the much feared southward march of PRC influence across the Malaysian land bridge prior to 1974, whether or not the PRC had such plans during this period. Will nationalism, bolstered by greater economic development and internal stability—albeit still an uncertainty—be sufficient to resist possible future PRC moves and any possible extension of Soviet influence across the land ridge between the Indian and Pacific oceans? The answer to this question, given an active Soviet policy in the area, hinges essentially on the rate and mode of economic and social development in the four countries, on their ability to work together in common defense, and on the policy and military-economic capability of the United States. The last factor could have a decisive effect on the first two.[252]

As of this writing, the United States has asserted that it has a continuing security interest in Southeast Asia. Only action in the area of the defense budget and of naval and air force build-up and deployment in the two oceans can offer visible evidence *to other nations,* however. Only a less ambivalent attitude toward such issues as collective regional defense, continued economic and military aid to South Vietnam, protection of the sea lanes to and from Japan, the future of Taiwan, and the development of secure energy and raw material supplies *both for itself and for its allies* can demonstrate that the Nixon Doctrine was not intended to be an euphemism for America's transition to a "number two power" on the downgrade.[253]

The United States has also asserted that it intends to substitute a larger economic presence for its military presence in Asia after the Vietnam War. But it has yet to demonstrate that its economic strength is not susceptible to external pressure, that this strength has not been sapped by worsening inflation, that it possesses an external economic policy consistent with its security policy, and that it knows how to avoid potential economic conflicts with countries it wishes to keep as allies or friends. Like the other major powers, the United States can no longer take its own credibility for granted. There is a need to acknowledge that this is a cost it has incurred—perhaps unwittingly—in the course of its policy shift because of its failure to appreciate fully the changing perceptions of its policy by others. Partly, however, since the world's strategic balance is not static, this is a cost inherent in a balance-of-power approach to foreign policy. The United States must learn to bear it. All these points need to be thought through by policy-makers before it is too late.

Notes

1. For a full discussion of the rationale of the "Nixon Doctrine" see the author's forthcoming volume, *U. S. Policy and Strategic Interest in the Western Pacific* (New York: Crane and Russak, in press).

2. Europe, of course, has found itself in the same state of disequilibrium.

3. The first rumblings of the Cultural Revolution (1966–69) were heard in the winter of 1965–66.

4. See the author's article on Japan's "oil diplomacy" in *Southeast Asia Spectrum* (in press).

5. On the strategic implications of the raw material issue, see Yuan-li Wu, *Raw Material Supply in a Multipolar World* (New York: National Strategy Information Center, 1973).

6. Japan declared on October 26, 1973, that Israel should withdraw from the territories it occupied during the 1967 war. The statement by Foreign Minister Masayoshi Ohira, reconfirmed by Chief Secretary of the Cabinet Susumu Nikaido, was couched in terms of the implementation of the 1967 UN resolution No. 242 which called for Israel's withdrawal. KYODO, Tokyo, November 6, 1973 .

7. UPI, Tokyo, January 1, 1974.

8. The reader should be reminded of the fact that while Japan's lifeline could be severed at the Malacca and Indonesian straits, disruption could also take place elsewhere. Hence the importance of the Taiwan Strait and the Bashi Channel between Taiwan and the Philippines.

9. One school of thought in the United States holds that the Soviet Union has no special naval ambitions in the Indian Ocean and that, if she did, the United States could do very little about it. The first point is, of course, conjectural and a matter of judgment. A policy planner cannot base contingency planning solely on "plausible" pleasant assumptions. The second point is defeatist. Even if true, however, should unpleasant possibilities be ignored without attempting to deal with them?

10. Some might prefer to view future developments in Thai external policy as a test of the "domino theory."

11. See, for example, the discussion of Chinese activities in Congo–Brazzaville, Mali, etc., in the unpublished study, Communist Military Assistance to Non-communist Developing Countries (Stanford, California: Hoover Institution, 1973).

12. As of 1974, there are signs of continuing power struggle in Peking and between Peking and regional authorities. Hence a third post-Mao and post-Chou phase may be in the offing.

13. These were set up in 1964 with headquarters in China. On December 14, 1965, the Thailand Independence Movement announced its affiliation with the Patriotic Front of Thailand (PFT).

14. According to the Front, beginning on August 7 the Thanom government had dispatched hundreds of armed police to Nakon Phanom, Nong Khai, and Ubon provinces in the northeast.

15. *The People's Daily*, September 10, 1965.

16. For a discussion on the attitude of villagers, see Somchai Rakwijit, *Village Leadership in Northeast Thailand*, November 1971, and *Study of Youth in Northeast Thailand*, April 1971, OSD/ARPA, R & D Center, Thailand.

17. *Bangkok World Supplement*, March 12, 1969.

18. *Bangkok Post*, March 19, 1969.

19. See the *Bangkok World*, March 21, 1969.

20. *Bangkok Post*, March 25, 1969. The same themes were stressed in an interview with this author in December 1970.

21. *Bangkok World*, afternoon supplement, March 25, 1969.

22. July 1, 1969.

23. See note 20.

24. NCNA, Peking, international service, February 15, 1971, quoting the "Voice of the People of Thailand" (VPT).

25. NCNA, February 17, 1971, again quoting the VPT in an article dated February 15, 1971, commemorating the tenth anniversary of the unification of the "South Vietnam People's Liberation Armed Forces."

26. See editorial in *Siam Rath*, Bangkok, February 19, 1971.

27. *Bangkok Post*, February 19, 1971.

28. Ibid., April 16, 1971.

29. According to the *Bangkok Post*, March 23, 1971, Hong Kong sources had reported Peking's invitation to businessmen from countries having no diplomatic relations with the PRC to apply for entry visas through the China Travel Service in Hong Kong. This invitation was interpreted to have included Thai businessmen.

30. Peking's initial response to Thai overtures, announced by Dr. Thanat in May 1971, can be interpreted as a probe to determine Thailand's position in the then forthcoming UN admission issue.

31. *Bangkok Post,* May 9, 1971.

32. May 14, 1971.

33. May 9, 1971.

34. VPT broadcast, May 8, 1971.

35. Bangkok radio, domestic service, May 12, 1971.

36. May 19, 1971.

37. Statement by Dr. Thanat on "Meet the Guest," a television program, as reported in the *Bangkok Post,* May 20, 1971.

38. Yet according to Praphat it was not Thai policy at that time to trade with Peking, at least not directly.

39. Statement by Charoon Sibunruang, president of the Thai Chamber of Commerce and of the Board of Trade, reported in *Bangkok Post,* May 4, 1971.

40. *Bangkok Post,* June 1, 1971.

41. Ibid., June 17, 1971. This proposal, advanced by the Malaysian Prime Minister Tun Abdul Razak, was discussed with Thanom Kittikachorn during the latter's visit to Kuala Lumpur in June 1971.

42. Ibid.

43. *The Nation,* Bangkok, July 15, 1971. The interview took place the previous day.

44. *Bangkok Post,* July 17, 1971.

45. Ibid., July 20, 1971.

46. This was advocated by Representative Yuang Lamsila of the United Thai People Party. Ibid., July 26, 1971.

47. See *The Nation, Bangkok,* July 26, 1971. The same party had long advocated relaxation of restrictions on travel to China and the opening of trade with Peking.

48. Ibid., July 26, 1971.

49. Asjeri in *Siam Rath* in Thai, Bangkok, July 19, 1971.

50. *Bangkok Post,* September 5, 1971.

51. VPT broadcast in Thai, July 15, 25, 1971.

52. *The Nation,* Bangkok, July 6, 1971.

53. Bangkok radio in Thai, September 6, 1971.

54. See the *Bangkok Post,* September 12, 1971, and *The Nation,* Bangkok, September 11, 1971.

55. *Bangkok Post,* September 16, 1971.

56. *The Nation,* Bangkok, September 21, 1971. Bunchana pointed to the danger of Chinese dumping of food and textiles in Thailand. He also noted that Thai exports to mainland China had been going indirectly through Hong Kong and Malaysia.

57. Ibid., September 25, 1971.

58. Broadcast by VPT in Thai, September 26, 1971.

59. As reported by Air Chief Marshall Thawi Chunlasap. See the *Bangkok Post,* October 25, 1971.

60. *Bangkok World,* October 25, 1971.

61. *The Nation,* Bangkok, October 27, 1971.

62. Ibid., October 17, 1971.

63. Ibid.

64. Ibid.

65. Ibid.

66. Cancellation of this parade was probably far more a consequence of the Lin Piao incident in mid-September, which had resulted in a serious political and military crisis in Communist China.

67. See the *Bangkok World,* October 26, 1971. The same position was repeated by Marshall Thanom in an interview on Bangkok radio in Thai November 1, 1971.

68. *The Nation,* Bangkok, October 27, 1971.

69. Ibid.

70. In particular, this required repeal of the late Prime Minister Sarit Thanarat's Revolutionary Party Announcement No. 53 which prohibited trade with mainland China.

71. *The Nation,* Bangkok, November 4, 1971.

72. *Bangkok Post,* November 11, 13, 1971.

73. Ibid., November 5, 1971.

74. Ibid., November 11, 1971.

75. Broadcast in Thai, November 22, 1971.

76. November 27, 1971.

77. VPT in Thai, November 24, 28, 1971; also *The Nation,* Bangkok, December 15, 1971.

78. *Bangkok Post,* December 7, 1971.

79. Bangkok radio in Thai, November 30, 1971. See also *Bangkok Post,* December 17, 1971, regarding guerrilla attacks on the Pon–Huay Khlon highway.

80. The report came from Nan Province near the Laotian border and 780 kilometers north of Bangkok. See *The Nation,* Bangkok, January 7, 1972.

81. *Bangkok World,* January 10, 1972.

82. Among the places mentioned were Nakhon Si Thammarat, Ubon Thani, Loei, Chiang Rai, Phitsanulok, Phetchabun, and Tak. VPT in Thai, February 6, 1972.

83. *Bangkok Post,* February 17, 1972.

84. Operation Phu Kwang under the 1972 Forward Joint Operations Command was launched in the Phitsanulok–Loei–Phetchabun border area at the beginning of February 1972. Bangkok radio in Thai, March 2, 1972.

85. In Thai, December 31, 1971.

86. February 17, 1972.

87. Incidentally, the same Phu Longkha area had been captured by government forces in 1968–69, only to be retaken by the insurgents. *Bangkok World,* March 17, 1972.

88. Bangkok radio in Thai, April 24, 1972.

89. *Bangkok World,* May 30, 1972. A Thai police estimate put the number of Chinese communist guerrillas in Songkhla, Yala, Pattani, and Narathiwat at one thousand. Ibid., May 25, 1972. A report of the *Bangkok Post,* July 27, 1972, mentioned Sib Termlin, a Chinese of Thai descent who was trained in Peking, as the leader of a communist camp in Na Saranplusri.

90. Bangkok radio, July 15, 1972, quoting a Revolutionary (government) Party release of July 11.

91. *Bangkok Post,* August 11, 1972. This was Announcement 199 of the Revolutionary Party issued on August 10, 1972 (BE 515).

92. Ibid., August 12, 1972.

93. Ibid., August 19, 1972.

94. *The Nation,* Bangkok, August 16, 1972.

95. Bangkok radio, August 18, 1972, quoting General Saiyud.

96. For instance, such a reduction in early September was reported by Bangkok radio on September 16, 1972.

97. Theh Chongkhadiki, *Bangkok Post,* October 4, 1972.

98. *Bangkok Post,* December 11, 1972.

99. Bangkok radio, November 24, 1972.

100. VPT in Thai, March 14, 1972.

101. Ibid.

102. In English, April 18, 1972.

103. For example, a roundup of activities since August was given on November 5 by VPT; the report covered all sections of the country.

104. In English, August 7, 1972.

105. In Thai, December 5, 1972.

106. See the *Bangkok Post,* May 19, 1972.

107. Bangkok radio, August 3, 1972.

108. *Bangkok World,* August 3, 1972.

109. *Bangkok Post,* August 5, 1972. Among the exiles in Peking, according to the *Post,* were Kularb Saipradist, a former president of the Press Association of Thailand; Payome Chulanon, a former MP from Pechaburi; and Mongkol Na Nakhon, also a politician. They were supposed to be working for Peking in directing insurgency in Thailand.

110. August 5, 1972.

111. Ibid.

112. *The Nation,* Bangkok, August 8, 1972.

113. Bangkok radio, August 10, 1972.

114. *Bangkok Post,* August 16, 1972.

115. Ibid.

116. Bangkok radio, August 16, 1972.

117. Ibid., September 15, 1972.

118. *Bangkok World,* September 15, 1972.

119. Ibid., October 5, 1972.

120. Bangkok radio in Thai, October 15, 1972.

121. *Bangkok Post,* December 11, 1972.

122. *People's Daily,* Peking, October 18, 1973. The student movement was described as "a just struggle."

123. The VPT stated on October 16, 1972: "The students *and* people will still have to join forces and pursue their struggle." On October 21 it noted that the new government did not represent "the people." On October 23 the King warned student leaders to guard against infiltration by outside powers. *Bangkok Post,* October 24, 1973.

124. The Air Marshall had previously received the PRC table tennis team during the latter's visit to Thailand in June 1973. NCNA, Bangkok, June 19, 1973.

125. *New York Times,* February 17, 1974, AP report from Bangkok.

126. NCNA, Peking, April 29, 1965. Note that Peking spoke of "Malaya" rather than "Malaysia," which it did not recognize.

127. Ibid., May 23, 27, 1965. Peking later accused Malaysia of depriving the population in "the Sarawak region of North Kalimantan" of its right to independence and of imprisoning eight thousand persons there in concentration camps under the pretext of protecting them from terrorists. This, said Peking, was carried out at British instigation. NCNA, Peking, July 31, 1965, quoting a commentator in the *Ta-kung Pao.*

128. NCNA, Peking, September 30, October 5, 15, 1965.

129. See the *Asian Almanac,* Singapore, May 9–15, 1965, p. 1116.

130. The threat to close the Bank of China in August was credited by Nan Han-chen, head of the People's Bank of China, to the Malaysian Minister of Finance, Tan Siew Sin, in a statement issued by Tan in Kuala Lumpur on June 12, 1965. See NCNA, Peking, June 27, 1965.

131. *Asian Almanac,* Singapore, August 1–7, 1965, pp. 1215–1216.

132. Ibid.

133. Ibid.

134. Singapore was admitted into the United Nations on September 21, 1965. Dr. Toh's statement was made prior to his departure for the UN. See ibid., October 24–30, 1965, p. 1313.

135. Statement of Inche Yusof, Head of State of the new nation, at the first Parliamentary Session. Ibid., December 12–18, 1965, pp. 1367–1368.

136. Ibid.

137. NCNA, Peking, August 13, 1965. Nan Han-chen called Singapore's decision to allow the Bank of China to continue operation in Singapore "beneficial to the development of the economy of Singapore" and "to the development of friendly relations between the peoples of Singapore and China." Note that there was no reference to friendly relations between the two governments.

138. Kuala Lumpur radio, January 24, 1969.

139. AST report from Singapore, March 7, 1969.

140. Kuala Lumpur radio, March 7, 1969.

141. Ibid., June 23, 1969. According to the Council, there were signs that some schools had been infiltrated by communists.

142. NCNA, Peking, February 17, 1969.

143. June 20, 1969.

144. According to Bin Dato Abu Samah, Malaysian Minister of Information and Culture, the VMR broadcasts originated from South China. *The Straits Times,* Singapore, October 3, 1970.

145. This first day broadcast was in Mandarin Chinese.

146. Such cases were reported by Kuala Lumpur radio on January 18, April 1 and 7, July 29, August 26, September 17, October 14, 27, 31, and November 18, 19, 20. Regarding Malaysian-Thai cooperation, agreement between the two sides was reportedly reached by Tun Razak and the Thai chief of staff in October 1969. The report stated that Malaysia promised to take firm measures against every Malaysian who supported or cooperated with the separatist movement in southern Thailand. Jakarta radio, October 19, 1969.

147. During 1969 guerrilla activities on both the Thai and the Indonesian borders of Malaysia were reported by NCNA, for instance, on February 11, March 23, July 31, August 11, September 6, October 26, 28, 31, and November 4. These announcements increased in frequency in 1970.

148. Kuala Lumpur radio, April 7, 1969.

149. The figure was given by the Thai air marshall who regarded a ten-to-one ratio of ground strength in favor of government forces as approaching the minimum necessary to eliminate the guerrillas. Melbourne overseas service, Kuala Lumpur, September 6, 1969.

150. For example, reports of guerrilla activities in Sarawak were given by Kuala Lumpur radio on April 3, August 7, 26, September 6, and November 20, 1969.

151. NCNA, Peking, January 4, 1970.

152. Ibid., March 4, 1970.

153. VMR broadcast in Mandarin Chinese to Malaysia and Singapore, April 26, 1970.

154. NCNA, May 23, 1970, quoting VMR of the previous day. During 1971 similar reports were contained in NCNA releases of May 20, 22, 27, June 10, 20, 21, July 6, 22, 28, August 13, and September 4.

Kuala Lumpur radio reports on terrorist activities were heard on January 6, 12, 13, 27, 30, March 2, 3, 7, 11, April 8, 20, 22, 30, May 13, 26, June 4, 22, July 16, 23, October 23, and November 18, 23, 1970. There seem to have been fewer such reports in 1971; however, either insurgent or counterinsurgency activities were mentioned on January 19, 21, 30, February 1, 13, 15, and May 15, 26.

None of the above listings is meant to be exhaustive; they are based on sampling.

155. NCNA, Peking, June 23, 1970, citing a statement of the People's Party in the June 1 issue of the *People's Tribune*, Singapore.

156. Broadcast in Mandarin Chinese to Malaysia and Singapore, June 30, 1971.

157. NCNA releases reporting insurgent activities in East Malaysia and on the Malaysian-Thai border were issued on January 6, 7, 14, February 12, 19, 25, March 5, 15, 25, April 16, 20, 23, May 22, 27, June 1, 8, 10, 20, 21, July 6, 20, 22, August 13, 30, September 4, October 25, and November 5, 1970.

158. NCNA, Peking, March 1, 1970, quoting a VMR article. The people's board of trust, of course, was a kind of operating mutual fund which provides the necessary scale to enter into joint ventures with foreign investors or to engage in modern undertakings on its own.

159. Ibid., April 15, 1970.

160. VMR broadcast in Mandarin Chinese to Malaysia and Singapore, May 30, 1970.

161. Ibid. in Mandarin Chinese, March 3, 1971. The attack was aimed at the Chinese Leaders' Symposium meeting in Kuala Lumpur at that time. In the past, Peking had defended the interests of Chinese businessmen in Indonesia who had no communist ties. The latter were not, however, open advocates of integration and identification with the host country.

162. Broadcast in Malay to Malaysia, January 19, 1970.

163. Ibid.

164. Ibid.

165. Report from Kuala Lumpur, dated September 30, 1970, by Bombay PTI. As late as mid-September 1970, Tunku Abdul Rahman, who was then Prime Minister, declared upon his return from a visit to Thailand that Peking was actively supporting insurgents on the Malaysian-Thai border and that there were frequent visits by Chin Peng, the Malayan Communist Party leader, to Peking. He also stressed the need to increase sea patrols to intercept movement of young Malaysian-Chinese recruits trying to join insurgents in Thailand. Kuala Lumpur radio, September 15, 1970.

166. See report from Bombay, note 165.

167. AFP dispatch from Singapore, October 3, 1970.

168. Ibid.

169. This view was advanced by Tun Razak in an address to a conference of police officers (Kuala Lumpur radio, October 15, 1970) and at a public rally in Kuantian (ibid., October 10, 1970).

170. AFP, Singapore, January 19, 1971.

171. Ibid., February 11, 1971.

172. Based on Razak's answer to a newsman's question. Kuala Lumpur radio, February 11, 1971.

173. AFP, Singapore, February 11, 1971.

174. Kuala Lumpur radio, February 19, 1971.

175. Ibid., March 10, 1971.

176. Ibid., March 12, 1971.

177. Ibid.

178. *The Straits Times*, Singapore, April 10, 1971.

179. Ibid., May 8, 1971.

180. Kuala Lumpur radio: several reports on May 19, 1971. Also on May 18.

181. Ibid., July 22, 1971.

182. This statement was made by Tan Sri Zaiton Ibrahim during an interview on Radio and Television Malaysia, May 26, 1971.

183. Kuala Lumpur radio, August 25, 28, 30, 1971.

184. Ibid., August 25, 1971.

185. Ibid., November 2, 1971.

186. This is a traditional popular Chinese story of a stupid thief.

187. Kuala Lumpur radio, September 6, 1971.

188. Ibid., September 19, 1971.

189. February 2, 1972, commemorating the 23rd anniversary of the founding of the "Malayan National Liberation Army."

190. Broadcast in Malay to Singapore and Malaysia, February 12, 1972.

191. Ibid.

192. VMR broadcast in Malay, May 10, 1972.

193. Ibid., May 31, 1972.

194. Kuala Lumpur radio, May 31, June 14, 19, August 28, September 5, October 3, December 5, 1972.

195. Ibid., December 5, 1972. The statement was made in answer to a question by Dr. Tan Chee Khoon of the Justice Party.

196. NCNA, Peking, January 5, February 16, March 29, April 22, May 4, 20, July 5, August 23, October 5, 1972.

197. Ibid., May 4, 10, 28, 30, September 3, 1972.

198. Ibid., March 13, 1972.

199. Kuala Lumpur radio, September 27, 1972.

200. Bombay PTI report in English, November 17, 1972.

201. A Republic of China consulate continued to function in Malaysia through the years until June 1974 when the reciprocal consular relationship was broken.

202. *People's Daily*, January 10, 1965. See also ibid., January 6, 1965. The immediate issue sparking the Indonesian withdrawal was the seating of Malaysia on the Security Council.

203. NCNA, Jakarta, January 10, 1965.

204. Ibid., Peking, January 11, 1965.

205. Ibid.

206. Ibid., January 24, 1965. Chou En-lai was addressing Subandrio, then Indonesian Foreign Minister, at a reception given in the latter's honor.

207. Ibid.

208. Ibid., January 12, 1965. Liu made the above statement while talking to the visiting Indonesian Minister of Air Communications, Iskandar.

209. Ibid., January 24, 1965.

210. Ibid., January 25, 1965.

211. Ibid. The term "old and new colonialism" was made current by Sukarno.

212. Ibid., September 29, 1965.

213. Ibid., September 30, 1965.

214. Ibid., October 2, 1965.

215. Ibid., October 19, 1965.

216. Ibid., October 7, 1965.

217. Protests were made by the PRC embassy on October 18, 25, November 4, 19, 26, 27, December 9, 15, 20.

218. The *Asian Analyst*, London, November 1965, p. 8. The allegations were, however, not followed up in subsequent reports.

219. Antara, October 25, 1965.

220. This was disclosed in Njono's confession as reported by the Indonesian Army Information Service. Njono was captured on October 3, 1965. See the *Asian Analyst*, London, December 1965, pp. 17–18.

221. The *Asian Analyst*, May 1967, pp. 11–13. Peking also has an intrinsic interest in winning the support of persons of Chinese ethnic origin who reside abroad. This is true of all past Chinese regimes.

222. Antara, Jakarta, August 19, 1969.

223. Ibid.

224. Ibid.

225. KAMI, Jakarta, June 17, 1970.

226. Ibid.

227. Antara, Jakarta, April 15, 1971.

228. Ibid.

229. Jakarta radio, quoting Adam Malik, April 24, 1971.

230. See Chapter 2.

231. *Merdeka,* Jakarta, September 8, 1971.

232. Jakarta radio, September 10, 1971.

233. *The New York Times,* October 27, 1971. Both Malaysia and Singapore voted against the U. S. resolution and in favor of the Albanian resolution.

234. NCNA, January 16, 23, 1971.

235. Jakarta radio, February 7, 1972.

236. Ibid., February 29, 1972. Statement by Domopranoto, Deputy Speaker of Parliament.

237. Japan might be added as an example of far greater nervousness in its response to the Shanghai communiqué.

238. Jakarta radio, August 6, 1972.

239. Ibid., September 11, 1972. Report on an interview given by the Indonesian Foreign Minister to a Saudi Arabian newsman.

240. Ibid., September 12, 1972.

241. Ibid., November 17, 1972.

242. Report by Shimomura in Japanese from Jakarta to the *Nihon Keizai,* Tokyo, September 22, 1972. Japan was then interested in improving its own relations with Peking and fearful lest the latter's terms might prove too severe. Japan was interested, therefore, in adding to its own bargaining chips.

243. Jakarta radio, September 30, 1972.

244. Ibid.

245. Radio Jakarta, September 3, 1972. The statement was made by Malik during an interview with a Radio Australia reporter.

246. Ibid., October 11, 1972.

247. Antara, Jakarta, November 3, 1972.

248. Ibid., December 13, 1972.

249. Jakarta radio, December 7, 1972.

250. Cf. the writings of Gurtov, formerly of the Rand Corporation.

251. The following are examples of development of Soviet and Eastern European contacts:

A Soviet–Thai trade agreement and a civil aviation agreement were concluded in 1971. (*Bangkok Post*, April 16, May 9, 1971.) The Soviet Union also entered the Thai fluorite market in 1971 in competition with Japan.

Malaysian businessmen were invited in 1969 to visit Moscow. (Kuala Lumpur radio, September 25, 1969.) A Soviet trade exhibition was held in Kuala Lumpur in September. A Soviet trade mission was sent to Sabah in December. (Ibid., December 16, 1969.) The Soviet Union also offered to establish joint ventures with Malaysians in thirty items.

During 1970, trade negotiations were held between Malaysia and Hungary, and a Malaysian-Bulgarian aviation agreement was signed. (Ibid., January 27, March 11, 1970.) A Malaysian-Bulgarian trade and technical cooperation agreement was concluded in June 1971. The establishment of direct shipping links with the Soviet Union was reported to be in the offing. (Ibid., April 15, 1971.) The first Pernas mission to Moscow to discuss rubber sales took place in July 1972. (Ibid., July 11, 1972.) A trade agreement was signed between Malaysia and Czechoslovakia in November. (Ibid., November 20, 1972.)

The first Soviet ambassador to Singapore arrived at his post on January 23, 1969. A civil aviation agreement was concluded in February involving the Aeroflot and the Malaysian-Singapore airline. A similar agreement was concluded with Czechoslovakia in July. A Bulgarian trade mission then appeared in Singapore in October. In 1971, the leader of the Soviet Merchant Marine delegation predicted that Soviet vessels would make Singapore their main port of call as Soviet trade expanded. (Singapore radio, April 29, 1971.)

In April 1971, the Soviet Union increased its purchase of Indonesian rubber as the PRC's purchase of Malaysian rubber increased. (Antara, April 26, 1971.) The Soviet Union has also expressed its willingness to resume abandoned aid projects in Indonesia in addition to rescheduling the repayment of Indonesia's outstanding debt.

252. This is not the place for a full discussion of these issues and U.S. interests. See, however, the author's forthcoming volume, *U. S. Policy and Strategic Interest in the Western Pacific* (New York: Crane and Russak, in press).

253. See note 252.

Index

Adjitorop, Jusuf, 64
Aeroflot routes, 74, 84 n. 251
Africa, 9, 17, 50, 59, 60, 62
Afro-Asian Solidarity, Chinese
    Committee for, 39
Aidit, D. N., 59, 63–64
Air Academy, Indonesia, 62
airbases, *see* military involvement
Albanian resolution (UN), 25, 26,
    52–53, 67, 88 n. 233
Alliance Party, Malaysia, 50
American Management Association
    Seminar, 18
Anti-communist Act (1952),
    Thailand, 22, 24, 28, 32, 37
Arab-Israeli War (1973), 5
Arab oil boycott (1973), 2–3, 7
Asia: U.S. in, 1, 6, 53, 59, 60, 75;
    collective security for, 17, 20, 74.
    See also by country
Asian Table Tennis Union,
    Chinese, 34
Australia, 4, 54
aviation, civil: Soviet, 48, 74,
    88 n. 251, 89 n. 251

badminton team, Indonesian, 66, 67
ballistic missile submarines, 5
Bandung Conference anniversary
    (1965), 19, 60
Bangkok Post, 20, 23, 28, 30, 35,
    78 n. 29
Bangkok World, 15, 20
Bank of China:
    Singapore branch, 40, 41,

83 n. 130, 83 n. 137
Banyat Tasaneyavig, 28
Barisan, Singapore, 43–44
Bashi Channel, 77 n. 8
Bay of Bengal: submarines in, 5
Black Sea: Soviet fleet in, 5
"board of trust, people's,"
    Malaysian, 47, 85 n. 158
Borneo: West, 45. *See also*
    Kalimastan
Breshnev, Leonid, 4
Bulgaria, 89 n. 251
Bunchana, Atthakar, 23, 26
Burma, 2, 18, 55
Buru Island: Chinese visitors to, 65

Cambodia, 13, 14
Canada, 50
Canton Trade Fair (1972), 36
cease-fire in Indochina: enforce-
    ment of, 5, 37, 73; signed, 10
Chen I, 19, 28–29, 39, 59, 61
Chen-pao, 16
China, Nationalists' Republic of:
    see Taiwan
China, People's Republic of:
    in rapprochment with U.S., 1, 2,
    8–11, 17, 25, 57, 62, 66, 73; as
    major power, 6–9, 72–74;
    Indonesia and, 6, 59–69, 89 n.
    251; and Soviet Union, 7–9, 11,
    15–17, 44, 48, 54, 55, 56, 74,
    89 n. 251; UN and, 11, 24–26,
    49–50, 52–53, 59, 60, 66; and
    Thailand, 13–37, 55, 60, 67,